THE MEALS IN A JAR

· HANDBOOK ·

with
Chef Tess
BAKERESSE

Gourmet Food Storage Made Easy

STEPHANIE PETERSEN

FRONT TABLE BOOKS | SPRINGVILLE, UTAH

ISBN 13: 978-1-4621-1378-1

Published by Front Table Books, an imprint of Cedar Fort, Inc.
2373 W. 700 S., Springville, UT 84663
Distributed by Cedar Fort, Inc., www.cedarfort.com

   Library of Congress Cataloging-in-Publication Data on file

Cover and page design by Erica Dixon
Cover design © 2014 by Lyle Mortimer
Edited by Casey J. Winters

Printed in China

10 9 8 7 6 5 4 3 2

To the Lord, for countless blessings and inspiration in the work of my life.

To my amazing husband, for being willing to sample a zillion freeze-dried meals without thinking his wife was too crazy.

To Auntie Em. You're still the wind beneath my wings.

Honeyville® FARMS™

⟨THE⟩

GOURMET
FOOD STORAGE

HANDBOOK

with
Chef Tess
BAKERESSE

STEPHANIE PETERSEN

CONTENTS

11 SKILLETS AND CASSEROLES

Contents

67 STEWS AND SOUPS

93 MEALS IN A JAR FOR ONE

103 BREAKFAST

127 BREAKFAST FOR ONE

143 BREADS

155 DESSERTS

173 HOLIDAY COOKIE MIXES

PREFACE

Over the last several years as a corporate chef, cooking instructor, TV chef, and radio personality, I've had the opportunity to meet people from all over the country. Every time I hear of a new friend using my "Meals in a Jar," my heart wants to sing! I've heard of my meals being used as wedding gifts, as care package additions to missionaries and troops, by new mothers, by aging parents, by individuals in assisted-living facilities, on camping trips for Boy Scouts, and in luggage to different countries all around the world. I'll never forget the first time I heard that one of these meals was being cooked in an underground shelter during a hurricane! "While the storm raged overhead, we were comforted by a warm stew simmering on the stove."

I've had many requests for a book devoted entirely to Meals in a Jar. For some people, using Meals in a Jar is about living a little simpler. For some it's about getting a bit more health conscious. Sometimes people simply need something to take to work to cook at the office. For others, it's about planning ahead for the unexpected job loss or calamity. Meals in a Jar have been put into action to feed my own family on many a busy weeknight. Many of these recipes are new to this book. You will not find them on the Internet. Some are from my previous publication, Honeyville's *The Gourmet Food Storage Handbook*, with updated directions, tips, and ingredients lists. These recipes are some of my favorites, and they are easily used for long-term emergency food storage or everyday use. All are made in a quart-sized jar unless indicated otherwise. I'm also including some of my breakfast choices as well as personal-sized meals for those who are cooking for one. Along with this, I'm including a few bread, muffin, and dessert recipes.

I hope you won't think of these meals as only being for emergencies because they are also for making your daily life just a little easier, healthier, and delicious. I know you'll find this to be the definitive resource for making your own shelf-stable Meals in a Jar. Enjoy!

INTRODUCTION TO THE "52 METHOD" FOR MEALS IN A JAR

"Meals in a Jar" has become one of my most popular classes at the Honeyville Teaching Kitchen. I love being the corporate chef for Honeyville Food Products and having the opportunity to create convenient menu plans using food storage and whole grain. I literally transform food storage items into meals a normal family will actually eat and enjoy. In this book, you will find the outline from the classes I teach, along with some new recipes never before shared in the Honeyville Kitchen. This is a Honeyville cookbook, so expect me to use their products exclusively! If you were reading the Pillsbury cookbook, you'd expect me to use their products, right? Well, this is Honeyville. We do things here for our customers and friends to make their lives easier. One of the things I do is provide amazing cookbooks!

As a chef in the restaurant industry, I planned food purchases based on a menu several times a week. I planned my family's dinner menus and purchases the same way. It makes sense to plan for longer-term storage based on a menu so that you are only purchasing things that you will need *and* love. All too often when people are planning their long-term food storage for emergencies, it is done with the mind-set that it is for a "rainy day," and if someone is hungry enough, they will eat what is stored. Truth be known, people—especially children—will starve to death rather than eat something that is unfamiliar to them. I wanted to store things in my pantry for long-term emergency use that my kids were familiar with and that I would feel good serving them should our emergency be something as simple as lack of employment. I didn't want to feed them high-sodium, flavorless wads of mush. Most of the meals I had tried that were made for food storage tasted the same way—awful!

I began with planning seven meals from my food storage, one for each night of the week based on a seven-day menu. From there I wanted to figure out how to get 52 of each meal from that seven-day menu for my food storage to have on hand. In this way I would easily have a year's supply of food that my family would eat should we need it. Initially I knew I could achieve this with 52 jars of spaghetti sauce and 52 pounds of spaghetti noodles if the meal was spaghetti on, say, Monday night for our family. It was a simple way to calculate a family's needs, as well

as getting back to the basics of what a normal family will eat. However, I quickly found living in a tiny condo and trying to remember where I had stored the sauce and the noodles became a problem. Several years into the project, getting the food storage and keeping track of cans and locations got tedious. Then I had a stroke of genius! One day when I was making soup mix, I put the entire contents of the mix into a quart-sized jar. I suddenly wondered why I had not planned my whole food storage this way. As time went on, that simple concept kept rising up in my mind. About that time, I found some Honeyville tomato powder at a food storage store in Arizona. (I was not yet their company chef.) It changed my life! Suddenly I realized I could make spaghetti dinner in one jar! Add the sauce and freeze-dried meat ingredients and the noodles together, and presto! Magic was born.

I had set criteria for my meals. First, I didn't want to go searching for the sauce and the noodles or any of the ingredients for a meal on my food storage menu. Next, the shelf-life needed to be around five to ten years. And the meals had to be simple enough that my kids could make them without my help. Seriously, what if something happened to me that kept me from being able to cook for the family? Could my kids walk into the pantry and know what to do with the cans that were lined up? At the time I started, the answer was "no way!" Now they can look at my cabinets and see exactly what is for dinner, grab a jar, and make a meal. Even my husband, who doesn't cook, could handle this task. He knows how to boil water and dump a jar of dry ingredients into the pot; I'll give him that much.

I took on a challenge, but I loved it! Over time, I started developing recipes that would allow me to fit everything for a meal into one quart-sized jar. I also wanted each meal to have only one rule—"just add water." I didn't want to have to find oil, butter, sugar, a can of tomatoes, or anything else. The first time I shared this concept with an emergency preparedness enthusiast, I got such a remarkable response that I decided maybe, just maybe, this would be something that others would use. This idea quickly spread to a lot of people who couldn't care less about emergency preparedness—they just wanted fantastic easy meals on hand for every day of the week!

I started looking in-depth at home canning safety. I didn't want to have to worry about canning meat or rotating cans of beans and vegetables. I cheered when I was introduced to freeze-dried fruits, meats, and vegetables along with the dehydration methods used for things like sour cream, egg crystallization, and butter. Hooray! I finally had all that I needed to really develop these meals! I've found that buying freeze-dried vegetables and meat has been a much better approach for our family than dehydrating them ourselves. It saves money to use the commercially made items, and when food is freeze-dried, 97 percent of the nutritional value of the food is preserved. It's a healthy way to approach food. It's a great way to avoid chopping, cooking, and prepping things yourself as well!

As I've fine-tuned my procedure, I've discovered using a widemouthed mason jar with a funnel is a tremendous help in adding the food items to the jars. All of the recipes in this book pretty much follow the same procedure for packing your meal in a jar. Always use the recommended-sized jar, and do not forget to top it with an oxygen absorber packet. You will see that in most of the recipes, I suggest shaking the loose items down into the bulkier items to make everything fit better in the jar. Just make sure you put the lid on first before you shake it!

INTRODUCTION TO MYLAR POUCH MEALS

Mylar pouches are lightweight bags used for long-term meal storage. Some people choose to do the Meals in a Jar using mylar bags if they live in earthquake zones. They also travel well in duffle bags or backpacks. If you are in need of quick, fast, and lightweight meals, using Mylar pouches is by far the easiest way to pack them.

First you will need to know what Mylar pouches are and where to get them. Essentially, the outside of the pouch is aluminum and the inside is lined with a food-grade plastic. Subsequently, when the outside of the bag is exposed to a strong enough heat, the plastic fuses together, causing a magnificent seal! For more information on how they are made and designed, visit sorbentsystems.com/mylar.html. I use and recommend the 5.0 millimeter food-grade pouches. They come in various sizes, but so far my favorite has been the 5-gallon size. They are available at all the Honeyville Farms retail and online locations. I've been able to cut the 5-gallon bag down to any size I want and maximize the cost effectiveness of the bag by making it into several personal- or family-size meal bags.

Second you will need oxygen absorber pouches. I also use them for Meals in a Jar, and they come in many different sizes. The size you use depends on the amount of food you will have in your Mylar bags. The 300cc absorbers are designed for 1-gallon bags. I use them for all of my personal and family-size meals, just so I don't have to buy a lot of different sizes. You *could* use a 50cc absorber for the personal-sized pouches, but I don't. The bags will suction around the food as the oxygen absorbers do their job. Don't be dismayed if a little air seems to be left in the bag. If you know your oxygen absorbers are viable and the seal on your bag was complete, you have nothing to worry about. Oxygen absorbers are designed to take out oxygen, not all the air. There will still be a small amount of nitrogen in the bag. Yes, even the smaller zip-bags sealed inside the Mylar will be okay. Twist them closed lightly—don't zip them. They will have their oxygen removed as well.

A word of caution: You *must* store your Mylar pouches with an oxygen absorber if you are using the real freeze-dried meat. These pouches are designed for long-term storage and will be fine for years (shelf life varies depending on the recipe) as long as you have the oxygen absorber.

Next you will require a hot iron. Machines for Mylar sealing *are* available—they are designed to get hot enough to create a perfect seal—but

I have found that a regular household iron seals the bags well. The iron must be used on the cotton setting without steam (see next page). A lot of people ask me if they can use a FoodSaver machine for the Mylar bags. So far, I have not had success with this. The machine doesn't get hot enough to fuse the bags together.

Mylar pouches are great in earthquake zones, but the disadvantage is that they are not rodent proof. Once you pack your bags, transfer them to a food-grade storage bucket or rodent-proof container. Those crazy mice will smell the delicious meals and come running!

HOME MYLAR POUCH SEALING PROCEDURE

* Set your iron on the cotton setting. No steam. Get a soft clean cloth and place it on your work surface or ironing board. The cloth protects your work surface from getting any melted plastic on it.

* After cutting the pouches to your desired size, iron the edges with the hot iron. Be sure that the edges are exactly aligned so that the plastic doesn't melt on your iron. Leave one side open for filling the pouches with food.

* Stack the cooled pouches while you prepare to fill them with your food. Avoid creasing in sharp folds. It can increase the chance of puncturing the bag.

* Fill the pouches with food. There are a few methods for this. I like putting the food in another bag inside the Mylar so it doesn't fall out of the bag when I'm sealing it. Obviously the more air that is removed, the better! I've had friends pack food inside FoodSaver bags, suction out the air, and then put them in the Mylar pouches.

* Once the Mylar pouches are filled with food, add the oxygen absorbers and seal. Work quickly. I recommend that you seal all the bags within 30–60 minutes from the time you open the oxygen absorbers, so keep that in mind.

* Next, label clearly! Make sure all pouches are labeled with contents, cooking instructions, and preparation date. Trust me, you will benefit greatly from knowing what is in the pouches.

* Finally, pack the Mylar pouches in food-grade buckets, backpacks, or travel bags as desired.

FREQUENTLY ASKED QUESTIONS

HOW DO I GET ALL THE INGREDIENTS TO FIT IN THE JAR?

Many times I include a lot more ingredients than one would think could fit in a jar. I shake the dry powder ingredients into the vegetables, grain, pasta, or meat. In this way, I'm not only able to reduce the amount of air in a jar, which will help with the shelf life, but I can also make the meal more compact for long-term storage. Shake the jars with the lids on. You'll be surprised how much will actually fit.

WHAT SIZE JAR SHOULD I USE?

Each recipe is intended for a quart-sized jar and will make 4 servings with plenty of food for each! I generally use a widemouthed mason jar, but these recipes can easily be cut in half and used for smaller families. I've done pint-sized jars for families with just two adults and had enough for dinner and then leftovers for the following day. Individual servings can be made in a half-pint jar. Simply adjust the cooking time and amount of water to account for these changes.

CAN I USE ZIP-SEALABLE BAGS OR OTHER PLASTIC BAGS FOR THESE MEALS FOR LONG-TERM STORAGE?

Zip-sealable bags are not designed for long-term storage. FoodSaver bags designed for use with a FoodSaver machine are also not designed for long-term storage. Thus, they are not recommended as the sole protection for repacking freeze-dried meats and cheeses because they are too porous for these purposes. However, I do use zip-sealable bags in my Meals in a Jar when storing the bags within the jars to keep products separate for later use, such as cheese for sprinkling on top after other ingredients are mixed. I also use zip-sealable bags for short-term storage when I make mixes like the hamburger skillet meals without freeze-dried meat.

CAN I USE DEHYDRATED VEGETABLES IN THESE RECIPES INSTEAD OF FREEZE-DRIED ITEMS?

Not always. I use different products for different cooking times and applications. Generally freeze-dried products cook completely differently and use a lot less water to hydrate than dehydrated items.

CAN I USE MY OWN HOME-DEHYDRATED ITEMS?

Should you use dehydrated vegetables you made at home, you will have to adjust cooking times, amount of water needed, and how much of each vegetable you use in the recipes. I cannot promise you will have the same results.

HOW DO I PREPARE AND LABEL EACH MEAL?

With each individual jar, I clearly label contents and include the cooking directions. I also include the date the meal was made. This label can be printed and affixed with tape to the jar or written on the lid of the jar with permanent ink. In this way, I always know what is in each jar and how to prepare it, and I also know the estimated shelf-life of the meal. This will ensure that each meal is useable and identifiable. There's nothing worse than looking at a Meal in a Jar and wondering if it's a dinner or dessert! "It could be meat. . . . It could be cake."

CAN I USE ANOTHER BRAND OF PRODUCTS FOR THESE RECIPES?

This is a Honeyville cookbook. I use their products not only because I'm their corporate chef but also because I'm consistently impressed with the quality of their products. Be aware that not all food storage is created equally! Some other companies use added sugars and preservatives and cut their products differently. Honeyville doesn't outsource to China for their ingredients. They are consistently non-GMO (except for some of their corn). As far as recipe cooking, smaller or larger pieces of carrot, for example, will have different cooking times and use a different amount of liquid to hydrate. Generally, this will also affect the quality of the finished recipes. In all cases, I am very product specific. The degree to which you follow my recipes is the degree to which you will have good results. These recipes use all Honeyville products for a reason: because they're outstanding!

WHAT DO YOU SERVE WITH YOUR MEALS IN A JAR?

Generally I plan a side dish to go with a meal during good times, and I always figure enough grain into my food storage to plan on 2–3 loaves of bread a day in addition to the jars. My family is used to baking bread from whole grain, and we eat fairly modestly. I also try to add fresh garden produce in the form of a salad whenever I can. However, in an extreme emergency, the jar meal is more than enough for my family.

IS THERE REALLY ENOUGH FOOD TO SERVE 4 TO 6 PEOPLE?

Yes! We have three adults and two teenage boys in my family and the quart-sized meals are usually more than generous for our family's needs. I'm sharing with you what has worked for us, so you'll need to try the meals yourself and plan accordingly. The jars will make 6–9 cups of cooked food, depending on the recipe.

DO YOU HAVE TO USE AN OXYGEN ABSORBER?

Oxygen "eater" packets are used to make meals shelf stable. These will cause an oxygen-free environment, which will keep out the growth of mold and spores. The lack of moisture is the key to the shelf stability of these meals. The jars should be packed in a dry jar on a day when the air has very low humidity. This is especially important when repacking freeze-dried meats. All of these meals will be stable for the estimated shelf life if stored in a cool, dry environment with an oxygen packet and in the instructed packaging.

Note: When using freeze-dried meat, it is important to open it and bottle it again within 24–48 hours in a very dry environment. If you're worried about it or want a vegetarian alternative, you can use 1½ cups of freeze-dried zucchini instead of the meat. You'll need to add 1 teaspoon of MSG-free chicken bouillon to the mix as well. It is not a good idea to seal these meals in just a plastic storage bag or one that is not designed for long-term storage if you are using the real meat. I'm especially conscious of that. Please don't risk getting your family sick. I can't be held liable for your bad choices.

SKILLETS AND CASSEROLES

DOUBLE CHEESEBURGER SKILLET

Estimated
Shelf Life
if stored in a cool, dry place

5–10
YEARS

This remarkably popular all-American meal is received with great enthusiasm most nights of the week! This version is made without cheese sauce powder, for those who want a totally natural version.

Jar ingredients:

½ cup Honeyville instant milk

½ cup Honeyville freeze-dried ground beef

2 cups Honeyville elbow macaroni

3 Tbsp. ultra gel* (modified cornstarch)

¼ cup Honeyville freeze-dried onion

½ cup Honeyville freeze-dried cheddar cheese

1 tsp. MSG-free beef bouillon

¼ tsp. turmeric

Jar directions: Layer ingredients in a widemouthed, quart-sized jar, shaking the dry powder ingredients into the bulkier items. Top with an oxygen packet for longer-term storage, cover with a new canning lid, and hand-tighten the metal ring.

Cooking directions: Remove oxygen packet and discard. Combine contents of the jar in a large skillet with 6 cups of hot water. Bring to a boil and cover. Simmer for 12–15 minutes until noodles are tender. Sauce will thicken a little more as it cools.

*NOTE: 2 tablespoons regular cornstarch can be used in place of the ultra gel, but be sure to bring to a boil when cooking.

STROGANOFF SKILLET

The addition of vinegar powder to this stroganoff gives it just the right amount of added tanginess and zip! You'll be pleasantly surprised by how simple it is to make.

Jar directions: Layer ingredients in a widemouthed quart-sized jar, shaking the dry powder ingredients into the bulkier items. Top with an oxygen packet for longer-term storage, cover with a new canning lid, and hand-tighten the metal ring.

Cooking directions: Remove oxygen packet and discard. Place contents of jar in a skillet. Add 6 cups of water and bring to a boil over high heat. Reduce the heat to a simmer and continue cooking for 12–15 minutes, stirring once or twice, but covering each time. When noodles are tender, season with salt and pepper if needed. Add more sour cream if desired as well.

*NOTE: 2 tablespoons regular cornstarch can be used in place of the Ultra Gel, but be sure to bring to a boil when cooking.

Estimated Shelf Life
if stored in a cool, dry place
5–10 YEARS

Jar ingredients:

- ½ cup Honeyville instant milk
- ½ cup Honeyville powdered sour cream
- 3 Tbsp. ultra gel* (modified cornstarch)
- ¼ cup Honeyville freeze-dried onion
- 1 tsp. MSG-free beef bouillon
- 2 cups Honeyville elbow macaroni or shell macaroni
- ½ cup Honeyville freeze-dried ground beef or sausage
- ½ cup Honeyville freeze-dried mushrooms
- 1 Tbsp. vinegar powder
- 1 tsp. dehydrated minced garlic
- $1/8$ tsp. black pepper
- 3 Tbsp. Honeyville powdered butter

BROCCOLI CHEESE AND RICE CASSEROLE

Estimated Shelf Life *if stored in a cool, dry place*

5–10 YEARS

Jar ingredients:

2 cups Honeyville long-grain rice

¼ cup Honeyville powdered butter

1 tsp. salt

Bag ingredients:

¼ cup Honeyville dehydrated celery

¼ cup Honeyville dehydrated onion

1 cup Honeyville freeze-dried broccoli

1 tsp. Chef Tess All-Purpose seasoning

½ cup Honeyville powdered cheese sauce

¼ cup Honeyville powdered butter

Converted from one of my family's favorite freezer meal recipes, this has become a staple at my house!

Jar directions: Put rice, butter, and salt in a wide-mouthed quart-sized jar. In a zip-sealable bag, add remaining ingredients. Squeeze out the air, twist closed, and place bag on top of ingredients in jar. Top with an oxygen packet for longer-term storage, cover with a new canning lid, and hand-tighten the metal ring.

Cooking directions: Remove oxygen packet and discard. Empty the contents of the bag into a quart-sized saucepan. Add 2 cups of water, bring to a boil, and reduce the heat. Simmer for 5–6 minutes. Turn off the heat and let sit for 5–6 minutes. While the sauce is cooking, place the rice in a quart-sized pot with a tight-fitting lid. Add 4 cups of boiling water or chicken stock. Cook covered on the lowest heat for 17–20 minutes until rice is tender. Spoon broccoli cheese sauce over rice and enjoy.

Broccoli Cheese
and Rice Casserole

CHEESE TURKEY NOODLE CASSEROLE

Estimated
Shelf Life
if stored in a cool, dry place

5–10 YEARS

Jar ingredients:

2 cups radiator or
   rotelle noodles

Bag ingredients:

¼ cup Honeyville
   freeze-dried broccoli

½ cup Honeyville
   freeze-dried mixed
   vegetable mix

1 cup Honeyville
   freeze-dried white turkey

½ cup Honeyville powdered
   cheese sauce

¼ cup Honeyville
   freeze-dried diced celery

1 Tbsp. Honeyville
   freeze-dried onion

1½ tsp. Chef Tess
   All-Purpose seasoning

Jar directions: Put the noodles in a widemouthed quart-sized jar. In a zip-sealable bag, add all remaining ingredients. Squeeze the air out of bag, twist closed, and place on top of the noodles in the jar. Top with an oxygen packet for longer-term storage, cover with a new canning lid, and hand-tighten the metal ring.

Cooking directions: Remove oxygen packet and discard. Empty the contents of the bag into a 2-quart saucepan. Add 2½ cups of water and bring to a boil. Boil for 5 minutes. Cover and turn off the heat. While sauce is cooking, bring 4 quarts of water to a boil in a gallon-sized saucepan and cook pasta for 10–12 minutes. When pasta is tender, drain. Stir into sauce mixture. Pour into casserole dish and top with additional cheese if desired.

SAUCY "BAKED" ZITI
WITH SAUSAGE AND MUSHROOMS

This dish quickly became my signature dish when it came to Meals in a Jar, not only because it is easy and delicious but also because everyone I know absolutely adores it!

Jar directions: Layer jar ingredients in a widemouthed quart-sized jar, shaking the dry powder ingredients into the bulkier items. In a small zip-sealable bag, add mozzarella cheese, twist close the seal, and place bag on top of ingredients in jar. Top with an oxygen packet for longer-term storage, cover with a new canning lid, and hand-tighten the metal ring.

Cooking directions: Remove oxygen packet and discard. Remove the bag and empty the contents of the jar into a skillet or pot with 4½ cups of water. Cover and simmer for 15–20 minutes until pasta is tender and sauce is thick. Empty the bag of cheese in a bowl and spray lightly with water. Let sit for 5 minutes. Uncover cooked pasta mixture. Top with cheese. Cover again and allow cheese to melt for about 5 minutes.

Jar ingredients:

- ⅔ cup Honeyville tomato powder
- ⅓ cup Honeyville dehydrated onion
- 1 Tbsp. Chef Tess romantic Italian seasoning
- ⅓ cup Honeyville freeze-dried sausage or sausage TVP
- ⅔ cup Honeyville freeze-dried ground beef
- 1 cup ziti or 3 oz. dry pasta of your choice
- ⅓ cup Honeyville freeze-dried mushroom

Bag ingredients:

- ⅓ cup Honeyville freeze-dried mozzarella cheese

CHEF TESS'S TURKEY NOODLE SKILLET

Estimated
Shelf Life
if stored in a cool, dry place

3–5 YEARS

My son will beg for this meal above all other Meals in a Jar. It has become his go-to whenever he wants to make a meal for himself. It is loaded with turkey and vegetables, so I know he's getting some great nutritious additions to his pasta.

Jar ingredients:

2 cups Honeyville egg noodles

½ cup Honeyville freeze-dried vegetable mix

⅓ cup Honeyville powdered cheese sauce

⅓ cup Honeyville instant milk

¼ cup Honeyville powdered butter

1 cup Honeyville freeze-dried white turkey

½ cup Honeyville freeze-dried mushroom slices

1 Tbsp. Honeyville dehydrated onions

1 tsp. Chef Tess romantic Italian seasoning

Jar directions: Layer ingredients in a widemouthed quart-sized jar, shaking the dry powder ingredients into the bulkier items. Top with an oxygen packet for longer-term storage, cover with a new canning lid, and hand-tighten the metal ring.

Cooking directions: Remove oxygen packet and discard. In a large skillet, empty contents of jar, add 3½ cups of hot water, and bring to a boil. Reduce the heat and simmer for 10–12 minutes, stirring every few minutes. Turn off the heat and let sit for 3–5 minutes. Sauce will thicken as it sits.

OAT AND BEEF PILAF WITH VEGGIES

A hearty meal that gives a whole-grain punch while still satisfying meaty cravings is a real gem! You'll love this filling and delicious dinner. Since it uses whole oats, plan for a longer cooking time.

Estimated Shelf Life *if stored in a cool, dry place* **10–15 YEARS**

Jar directions: Layer ingredients in a widemouthed quart-sized jar, shaking the dry powder ingredients into the bulkier items. Top with an oxygen packet for longer-term storage, cover with a new canning lid, and hand-tighten the metal ring.

Cooking directions: Remove oxygen packet and discard. Combine all ingredients in a 4-quart covered pot. Add 8 cups of water and simmer on low, covered, for 90 minutes. (This meal is also excellent in a slow cooker, but use 7 cups of water instead and cook on high for 2–3 hours or low for 4–5 hours.)

Jar ingredients:

- 2 cups whole-grain oat groats or pearl barley
- 1 cup Honeyville freeze-dried beef
- 1 Tbsp. Chef Tess All-Purpose seasoning
- 1 Tbsp. MSG-free beef bouillon
- ½ cup Honeyville freeze-dried vegetable mix
- ⅓ cup Honeyville freeze-dried onion
- 1½ tsp. dehydrated minced garlic

Beefy Taco Rice

BEEFY TACO RICE

I grew up with taco rice that my dad made when my mom was at work or he wanted a simple meal. Every single time I make this, I think of my dad.

Jar directions: Layer ingredients in a widemouthed quart-sized jar, shaking the dry powder ingredients into the bulkier items. Top with an oxygen packet for longer-term storage, cover with a new canning lid, and hand-tighten the metal ring.

Cooking directions: Remove oxygen packet and discard. Add contents of jar to 5½ cups of boiling water. Cover and simmer on low for 25–30 minutes until tender. Top with cheese or sour cream if desired.

Estimated Shelf Life
if stored in a cool, dry place

5–10 YEARS

Jar ingredients:

½ cup Honeyville freeze-dried ground beef or beef TVP

1½ cups Honeyville parboiled rice

½ cup Honeyville freeze-dried bell pepper

½ cup Honeyville dehydrated onion

1 Tbsp. Chef Tess Southwest Fajita seasoning

1 tsp. dehydrated minced garlic

1 Tbsp. dehydrated minced ancho chilies

1½ tsp. salt

½ tsp. smoked paprika

¼ cup Honeyville tomato powder

1 bay leaf

2 tsp. MSG-free beef bouillon

BEAN AND RICE FAJITA CASSEROLE

Estimated
Shelf Life
if stored in a cool, dry place

5–10 YEARS

Jar ingredients:

2 cups Honeyville quick cook
red or black beans

1 cup Honeyville long-grain
rice

½ cup Honeyville
freeze-dried bell pepper

½ cup Honeyville
dehydrated onion

1 Tbsp. Chef Tess
All-Purpose seasoning

½ tsp. cumin seed

½ tsp. dehydrated oregano
leaves (or 1 drop oil of
oregano)

1 tsp. dehydrated minced
garlic

1 dehydrated bay leaf

½ cup Honeyville powdered
cheese sauce

¼ cup Honeyville tomato
powder

This isn't the typical beans and rice dinner. You'll be pleasantly surprised at the creamy cheesy sauce and the bold flavor.

Jar directions: Layer ingredients in a widemouthed quart-sized jar, shaking the dry powder ingredients into the bulkier items. Top with an oxygen packet for longer-term storage, cover with a new canning lid, and hand-tighten the metal ring.

Cooking directions: Remove oxygen packet and discard. Empty contents of jar into a deep, covered casserole dish and add 6 cups of very hot water. Place covered dish in conventional oven and bake for 30–35 minutes at 350°F.

Bean and Rice
Fajita Casserole

SAUSAGE AND APPLE OAT STUFFING

Estimated
Shelf Life
if stored in a cool, dry place

10–15 YEARS

Jar ingredients:

1 cup Honeyville freeze-dried sausage

1 cup Honeyville steel-cut oats

1 cup Honeyville freeze-dried apples

¼ cup Honeyville freeze-dried bell peppers

¼ cup Honeyville dehydrated onion

¼ cup Honeyville powdered butter

1 tsp. Chef Tess French Provencal Essential seasoning

¼ tsp. black pepper

2 Tbsp. MSG-free chicken bouillon (optional)

This is a hearty sausage stuffing with the classic combining of apple for a sweet and savory delight.

Jar directions: Layer ingredients in a widemouthed quart-sized jar, shaking the dry powder ingredients into the bulkier items. Top with an oxygen packet for longer-term storage, cover with a new canning lid, and hand-tighten the metal ring.

Cooking directions: Remove oxygen packet and discard. Preheat oven to 350 degrees. Combine all ingredients with 6 cups of hot water in a 4-quart casserole dish with a lid. Bake covered in a preheated oven at 350°F for 1 hour.

YANKEE POT ROAST GRAVY
OVER MASHED POTATOES

This is a man's meal. It is meat and potatoes with emphasis on the meaty meat. Don't use textured vegetable protein here—it won't be the same.

Jar directions: Layer jar ingredients in the bottom of a widemouthed quart-sized jar, shaking the dry powder ingredients into the bulkier items. In a sandwich-sized zip-sealable bag, add remaining ingredients. Squeeze air out of the bag, zip seal, and place in jar. Top with an oxygen packet for longer-term storage, cover with a new canning lid, and hand-tighten the metal ring.

Cooking directions: Remove oxygen packet and discard. Empty the entire contents of the bag into a bowl. Empty the jar ingredients into a 2-quart saucepan. Add 4 cups of very hot water to the pot and stir well. Place on stove and bring to a simmer for 15–20 minutes. Turn off the heat and leave covered for an additional 5 minutes. While the gravy sets, bring 2 cups of water to a boil in a separate saucepan, then pour in the bag contents, stirring well. Serve the gravy over the potatoes.

*NOTE: ¼ cup regular cornstarch can be used in place of the ultra gel, but be sure to bring to a boil when cooking.

Jar ingredients:

2 cups Honeyville freeze-dried diced beef

¼ cup ultra gel* (modified cornstarch)

¼ cup Honeyville freeze-dried mushroom

⅓ cup Honeyville dehydrated onion

2 tsp. MSG-free beef bouillon

1 tsp. dehydrated minced garlic

1 tsp. Chef Tess All-Purpose seasoning

1 Tbsp. Honeyville tomato powder

Bag ingredients:

1½ cups Honeyville potato flakes

1 tsp. granulated garlic

3 Tbsp. Honeyville powdered butter

Estimated Shelf Life
if stored in a cool, dry place
5 YEARS

FRUITED CREAMY CHICKEN WITH RICE PILAF

Estimated Shelf Life
if stored in a cool, dry place

5–10 YEARS

Jar ingredients:

1½ cups Honeyville long-grain rice

¼ cup Honeyville dehydrated carrots

½ cup Honeyville freeze-dried mushrooms

2 Tbsp. Honeyville dehydrated onion

2 Tbsp. Honeyville dehydrated celery

½ cup Honeyville freeze-dried apricots or apples

1 cup Honeyville powdered sour cream

¼ cup Honeyville powdered butter

1 cup Honeyville freeze-dried chicken

1 tsp. dry thyme

1 tsp. poultry seasoning

½ tsp. pepper

Jar directions: Layer ingredients in a widemouthed quart-sized jar, shaking the dry powder ingredients into the bulkier items. Top with an oxygen packet for longer-term storage, cover with a new canning lid, and hand-tighten the metal ring.

Cooking directions: Remove oxygen packet and discard. Combine all ingredients in a 4-quart pot with 5½ cups of water and simmer on low heat for 20–25 minutes until rice is tender.

MANGO TANGY TEXAS BEEF AND BEANS

Round 'em up, because dinner just went to Texas! This is a savory and fillin' country-style barbecue bean with a lot of beef and the surprisingly delightful addition of mango!

Estimated Shelf Life
if stored in a cool, dry place

10 YEARS

Jar Directions: Layer ingredients in a widemouthed quart-sized jar, shaking the dry powder ingredients into the bulkier items. Top with an oxygen packet for longer-term storage, cover with a new canning lid, and hand-tighten the metal ring.

Cooking Directions: Remove oxygen packet and discard. In a saucepan, combine jar ingredients and 5½ cups of water and simmer on low for 15–20 minutes until beans are tender.

*SHIRLEY J BARBECUE SAUCE MIX can be found at Honeyville retail locations, or regular barbecue sauce powder can be found at firehousepantrystore.com.

Jar ingredients:

1 cup Honeyville freeze-dried diced beef

1½ cups Honeyville quick cook red beans

½ cup Honeyville dehydrated onion

½ cup Honeyville freeze-dried mango

½ cup Honeyville freeze-dried bell pepper

½ cup Honeyville tomato powder

½ cup barbecue sauce mix*

1 tsp. celery seed

1 Tbsp. chili powder

½ tsp. pepper

1 pinch cayenne pepper (optional)

HUNGARIAN BEEF PAPRIKASH WITH RICE

Jar ingredients:

1½ cups Honeyville freeze-dried diced beef

½ cup Honeyville dehydrated onion

½ cup Honeyville freeze-dried mushroom

¼ cup Honeyville all-purpose flour

¼ cup Honeyville powdered butter

¼ cup Honeyville powdered sour cream

¼ cup Honeyville tomato powder

¼ tsp. baking soda

¼ cup Honeyville freeze-dried bell pepper

1 tsp. dry thyme

1 Tbsp. Hungarian paprika

Bag ingredients:

1 cup Honeyville long-grain rice

This recipe is made with beef, but you can easily make a chicken paprikash by using Honeyville freeze-dried chicken instead of the beef!

Jar directions: Layer jar ingredients in a widemouthed quart-sized jar, shaking the dry powder ingredients into the bulkier items. In a zip-sealable bag, add rice. Squeeze air out of the bag, twist bag closed, and place on top of the other ingredients. Top jar with an oxygen packet for long-term storage, cover with a new canning lid, and hand-tighten the metal ring.

Cooking directions: Remove oxygen packet and discard. In a saucepan, add the meat mixture and 5 cups of water and simmer on low for 15–20 minutes until beef is tender. In a 1-quart saucepan, add 2 cups of water and the contents of the bag of rice. Bring to a boil. Reduce the heat to low and cover with a tight lid. Simmer for 20 minutes while the beef mixture cooks. Serve the rice with a hearty scoop of the beef mixture.

Estimated Shelf Life *if stored in a cool, dry place* **10 YEARS**

POLYNESIAN ORANGE-GLAZED CHICKEN WITH COCONUT RICE

This was once a favorite slow cooker recipe, but now it has been converted into a favorite quick-cooking recipe! This one uses a little more meat than the rest of my recipes, but it is full of tropical flavors.

Jar directions: Layer jar ingredients in a widemouthed quart-sized jar, shaking the dry powder ingredients into the bulkier items. In a zip-sealable bag, add the bag ingredients. Squeeze air out of the bag, zip seal, and place in the jar. Top jar with an oxygen packet for long-term storage, cover with a new canning lid, and hand-tighten the metal ring.

Cooking directions: Remove oxygen packet and discard. Remove bag. Add 4 cups of water to a saucepan, add the jar ingredients, and simmer on low for 15–20 minutes. In a separate saucepan, add 2 cups of water and the contents of the bag. Bring to a boil, and simmer covered on low for 15–20 minutes. Serve the chicken mixture over the rice.

*NOTE: Vinegar powder, soy sauce powder, and coconut powder flavor are available at Honeyville retail stores, or online at other locations.

Estimated Shelf Life
if stored in a cool, dry place
10–15 YEARS

Jar ingredients:

- 2 cups Honeyville freeze-dried white chicken
- ½ cup Honeyville freeze-dried mango or pineapple
- ¼ cup dehydrated onion
- ¼ cup Honeyville freeze-dried bell pepper
- ¼ cup sugar or granulated honey
- 2 Tbsp. green onion
- 1 tsp. ground ginger
- 1 Tbsp. dehydrated orange zest
- 2 Tbsp. vinegar powder*
- ¼ cup soy sauce powder*
- 2 tsp. dehydrated minced garlic

Bag ingredients:

- 1 cup jasmine or Honeyville long-grain rice
- 1 tsp. coconut powder flavor*
- 1 tsp. granulated garlic
- 1 tsp. granulated onion
- 2 tsp. MSG-free chicken bouillon

Creamy Chicken
Veggie Casserole

CREAMY CHICKEN VEGGIE CASSEROLE

Unlike previous recipes where you have to cook the pasta separately, you can make this meal all in one pot. It is perfect for camping or Dutch oven baking!

Estimated Shelf Life
if stored in a cool, dry place
5–10 YEARS

Jar directions: Layer ingredients in a widemouthed quart-sized jar, shaking the dry powder ingredients into the bulkier items. Top with an oxygen packet for longer-term storage, cover with a new canning lid, and hand-tighten the metal ring.

Cooking directions: Remove oxygen packet and discard. In a casserole dish, combine the entire contents of the jar with 4 cups of hot water. Let sit for 5 minutes. Cover and bake in a preheated oven at 350°F for 30–35 minutes or microwave in a covered, deep casserole dish for 15 minutes.

Jar ingredients:

1¾ cups egg noodles

½ cup Honeyville freeze-dried vegetable mix

1 cup Honeyville freeze-dried white chicken

½ cup Honeyville freeze-dried peas

¼ cup Honeyville freeze-dried mushroom slices

2 Tbsp. Honeyville dehydrated onions

1 tsp. Chef Tess romantic Italian seasoning

½ cup Honeyville powdered cheese sauce

⅓ cup Honeyville instant milk

⅓ cup Honeyville powdered sour cream or cream cheese powder

¼ cup Honeyville powdered butter

GOLDEN POTATO, CHEESE, AND SAUSAGE CASSEROLE

Estimated Shelf Life
if stored in a cool, dry place
5–10 YEARS

Jar ingredients:

- 1 cup Honeyville freeze-dried sausage (or ham)
- 2 cups (4 oz.) Honeyville dehydrated hash brown potatoes
- 1 cup Honeyville powdered cheese sauce
- ½ cup Honeyville sour cream powder or cream cheese powder
- ⅓ cup Honeyville dehydrated onion
- 1½ tsp. dehydrated minced garlic
- ⅛ tsp. ground nutmeg
- ½ tsp. cracked fresh pepper

I grew up in the great state of Utah, where this creamy potato casserole was served at church potlucks and at funerals. We actually called them "Funeral Potatoes" when I was a kid! They're the ultimate comforting casserole—and nobody has to die for you to enjoy them. There are as many variations of this recipe as there are cooks in the state of Utah, but this is my family's favorite version.

Jar directions: Layer ingredients in a widemouthed quart-sized jar, shaking the dry powder ingredients into the bulkier items. Top with an oxygen packet for longer-term storage, cover with a new canning lid, and hand-tighten the metal ring.

Cooking directions: Remove oxygen packet and discard. Combine ingredients in a deep casserole dish with 5½ cups of hot water. Cover for 10 minutes. Bake covered in a preheated oven at 350°F for 1 hour or in the microwave on high, uncovered, for 15 minutes. Top with additional cheese, crushed corn flakes, or crushed crackers if desired.

Golden Potato, Cheese, and Sausage Casserole

SOUTHERN-STYLE CREAMED CORN AND SAUSAGE

Estimated
Shelf Life
if stored in a cool, dry place

5–10 YEARS

I think the ultimate sweet and savory combination has got to be corn and sausage. The first time I tasted Honeyville freeze-dried corn, I was transported by its sweet flavor to my childhood. Dad would grow corn in the family garden, and I could often be found hiding in the tall stalks, sitting in the dirt, with my cute little-girl hands wrapped around a freshly shucked corn cob. I loved that sweet flavor.

Jar ingredients:

¼ cup Honeyville powdered butter

½ tsp. salt

½ tsp. Chef Tess Romantic Italian seasoning

1 Tbsp. Honeyville granulated honey

2 Tbsp. Honeyville cornmeal

½ cup Honeyville powdered sour cream

2 Tbsp. Honeyville dehydrated green onion

fresh-ground black pepper

3 cups Honeyville freeze-dried corn

¼ cup Honeyville freeze-dried sausage or TVP sausage

Jar directions: Layer ingredients in a widemouthed quart-sized jar, shaking the dry powder ingredients into the bulkier items. Top with an oxygen packet for longer-term storage, cover with a new canning lid, and hand-tighten the metal ring.

Cooking directions: Remove oxygen packet and discard. Combine all ingredients in a medium heavy pot. Add 4 cups of hot water and stir over medium heat for about 20 minutes until cooked through and tender.

POLYNESIAN SWEET-AND-SOUR CHICKEN BAKED BEANS

This unique twist on the traditional baked bean recipe will add some great variety to your evening meals. Every time I've shared this one with my students, there has been a lot of excitement and surprise at how easy it is to make and how delightful it is to eat!

Estimated Shelf Life *if stored in a cool, dry place* — **10 YEARS**

Jar directions: Layer ingredients in a widemouthed quart-sized jar, shaking the powdered ingredients in before adding the bell peppers and pineapple. Top with an oxygen packet for longer-term storage, cover with a new canning lid, and hand-tighten the metal ring.

Cooking directions: Remove oxygen packet and discard. In a saucepan, add jar ingredients and 5 cups of water and simmer on low for 30 minutes.

*NOH HAWAIIAN-STYLE TERI-BURGER MIX is available at Asian and Polynesian markets and online.

**CHECK OUT www.firehousepantrystore.com for vinegar powder.

***NOTE: 2 tablespoons regular cornstarch can be used in place of the ultra gel, but be sure to bring to a boil when cooking.

Jar ingredients:

- 2 cups Honeyville quick cook red beans
- 1 cup Honeyville freeze-dried white chicken or chicken TVP
- ¼ cup Honeyville dehydrated onion
- 1 (1½-oz.) pkg. NOH Hawaiian-style teri-burger meatloaf seasoning mix*
- 2 Tbsp. vinegar powder**
- ¼ cup Honeyville granulated honey
- 1 Tbsp. dehydrated minced garlic
- 2 Tbsp. ultra gel*** (modified cornstarch)
- ½ cup Honeyville freeze-dried bell peppers
- ½ cup Honeyville freeze-dried pineapple

Hawaiian-Style Teriyaki Beef and Vegetables with Rice

HAWAIIAN-STYLE TERIYAKI BEEF AND VEGETABLES WITH RICE

This recipe uses a teriyaki meatloaf seasoning. I think the flavor is outstanding.

Jar directions: Layer jar ingredients in a widemouthed quart-sized jar, shaking the dry powder ingredients into the bulkier items. In a zip-sealable bag, add rice. Squeeze air out of the bag, twist closed, and place in jar. Top jar with an oxygen packet for longer-term storage, cover with a new canning lid, and hand-tighten the metal ring.

Cooking directions: Remove oxygen packet and discard. In a medium saucepan with a tight-fitting lid, add 2 cups of water and the bag contents. When the rice and water come to a boil, reduce the heat to very low and simmer for 20 minutes. In a separate saucepan, add 3½ cups of very hot water and the jar ingredients. Allow to sit for 10 minutes to absorb water. Place on stove and turn to medium heat, cooking 5–7 minutes more until sauce has slightly thickened. The rice and sauce will be finished cooking at about the same time if you cook them simultaneously.

*NOH HAWAIIAN-STYLE TERI-BURGER MIX is available at Asian and Polynesian markets and online.

**NOTE: 2 tablespoons regular cornstarch can be used in place of the ultra gel, but be sure to bring to a boil when cooking.

Estimated Shelf Life
if stored in a cool, dry place
7–10 YEARS

Jar ingredients:

1 cup Honeyville freeze-dried diced beef

1 cup Honeyville freeze-dried broccoli

¾ cup Honeyville freeze-dried bell pepper

¼ cup Honeyville freeze-dried onion or dehydrated green onion

1 (1½-oz.) pkg. NOH Hawaiian-style teri-burger meatloaf seasoning mix*

2 Tbsp. ultra gel** (modified cornstarch)

Bag ingredients:

1 cup Honeyville long-grain or parboiled rice

CHEESY HAM AND PEA PASTA

Estimated
Shelf Life
if stored in a cool, dry place

2
YEARS

Jar ingredients:

12 oz. dry small cheese
tortellini

½ cup Honeyville instant
milk

½ cup Honeyville powdered
sour cream

3 Tbsp. ultra gel*
(modified cornstarch)

¼ cup Honeyville
freeze-dried onion

1 tsp. MSG-free beef
bouillon

½ cup Honeyville
freeze-dried peas

¾ cup Honeyville
freeze-dried ham

1 tsp. Chef Tess romantic
Italian seasoning

This meal has a shorter shelf life than the other recipes because of the dried tortellini, but it tends to fly off the shelves around here. I wouldn't expect it to stick around very long if your family knows it is in the house!

Jar directions: Layer ingredients in a widemouthed quart-sized jar, shaking the dry powder ingredients into the bulkier items. Top with an oxygen packet for longer-term storage, cover with a new canning lid, and hand-tighten the metal ring.

Cooking directions: Remove oxygen packet and discard. In a saucepan, boil 6 cups of water. Add ingredients from jar and boil for 15–17 minutes until pasta is tender.

*NOTE: 3 tablespoons regular cornstarch can be used in place of the ultra gel, but be sure to bring to a boil when cooking.

CHICKEN AND SWEET POTATO WITH CITRUS SAUCE AND RICE

This has all the flavors of a festive holiday dinner, all in one dish!

Estimated
Shelf Life
if stored in a cool, dry place

10–15 YEARS

Jar directions: Layer jar ingredients in a widemouthed quart-sized jar, shaking the dry powder ingredients into the bulkier items. In a zip-sealable bag, add the bag ingredients. Squeeze out the air, zip seal, and place bag in jar. Top with an oxygen packet for longer-term storage, cover with a new canning lid, and hand-tighten the metal ring.

Cooking directions: Remove oxygen packet and discard. In a quart-sized saucepan, add 2 cups of water and the contents of the bag. Bring to a boil and then simmer, covered, on low for 20 minutes. In a separate pot, combine the jar ingredients with 4 cups of water and simmer until the chicken and potatoes are tender, about 20–25 minutes.

*NOTE: ¼ cup regular cornstarch can be used in place of the ultra gel, but be sure to bring to a boil when cooking.

Jar ingredients:

- 1 cup Honeyville freeze-dried white chicken

- 1 cup Honeyville freeze-dried sweet potato

- 2 tsp. dehydrated orange zest

- ½ tsp. Chef Tess Wise Woman of the East spice blend

- ¼ cup ultra gel* (modified cornstarch)

- 2 Tbsp. Honeyville lemonade powder

- 2 tsp. MSG-free chicken bouillon

Bag ingredients:

- 1 cup Honeyville long-grain rice

- 1 tsp. curry powder

- 2 tsp. MSG-free chicken bouillon

CAJUN RED BEANS, SAUSAGE, AND RICE

Jar ingredients:

½ cup Honeyville
freeze-dried sausage or
sausage TVP

1½ tsp. dehydrated minced
garlic

½ tsp black pepper

2 tsp. hot sauce powder

½ tsp. thyme

1 tsp. smoked paprika

¼ tsp. dry rubbed sage

¼ tsp. hickory smoke powder

⅓ cup Honeyville
dehydrated onion

½ cup Honeyville
freeze-dried bell peppers

¼ cup dehydrated celery

1 cup Honeyville quick-cook
red beans

1 tsp. MSG-free Chicken
bouillon

Bag ingredients

1 cup Honeyville
long-grain rice

1 tsp. salt

Jar directions: Layer jar ingredients in a widemouthed quart-sized jar, shaking the dry powder ingredients into the bulkier items. In a zip-sealable bag, add the bag ingredients. Squeeze out the air, zip seal, and place bag in jar. Top with an oxygen packet for longer-term storage, cover with a new canning lid, and hand-tighten the metal ring.

Cooking directions: Remove oxygen packet and discard. In a quart-sized saucepan, add 2 cups of water and the contents of the bag. Bring to a boil and then simmer, covered, on low for 20 minutes. In a separate pot, combine the remaining jar ingredients with 4 cups of water and simmer until the beans are tender, about 20–25 minutes. Serve over the rice.

Estimated
Shelf Life
if stored in a cool, dry place

**5–10
YEARS**

Cajun Red Beans, Sausage, and Rice

NACHO POTATOES AND BEEF SKILLET CASSEROLE

Estimated
Shelf Life
if stored in a cool, dry place

5–10 YEARS

South-of-the-border taste with familiar ingredients are the key to a really good Mexican casserole. This recipe uses ancho chili powder. It is also called pasilla chili pepper by those who love it most. I just call it "awesome"! This pepper can be found in many Mexican markets or in the spice section of many grocery stores.

Jar ingredients:

- 1 cup Honeyville freeze-dried ground beef
- 2 cups Honeyville dehydrated hash brown potatoes
- 1 cup Honeyville powdered cheese sauce
- ½ cup Honeyville sour cream powder or cream cheese powder
- ⅓ cup Honeyville dehydrated onion
- 1½ tsp. dehydrated minced garlic
- 1½ Tbsp. ancho chili powder
- 1 Tbsp. Chef Tess Southwest Fajita seasoning
- ⅛ tsp. allspice
- ½ tsp. cracked fresh pepper

Jar directions: Layer ingredients in a widemouthed quart-sized jar, shaking the dry powder ingredients into the bulkier items. Top with an oxygen packet for longer-term storage, cover with a new canning lid, and hand-tighten the metal ring.

Cooking directions: Remove oxygen packet and discard. Combine ingredients with 5½ cups of hot water in a deep casserole dish. Cover for 10 minutes. Bake covered in a pre-heated oven at 350°F for 1 hour or in the microwave uncovered on high for 15 minutes. Top with additional cheese, crushed corn flakes, or crushed crackers if desired.

CHEESY SCALLOPED POTATOES AND HAM

This all-American classic just got super simple!

Jar directions: Layer ingredients in a widemouthed quart-sized jar, shaking the dry powder ingredients into the bulkier items. Top with an oxygen packet for longer-term storage, cover with a new canning lid, and hand-tighten the metal ring.

Cooking directions: Remove oxygen packet and discard. Combine jar ingredients with 6 cups water in a 12-inch, deep skillet with a lid. Stir well and bring to a slow boil over medium heat. Once boiling, lower heat to very low for 12–15 minutes, uncovered. Stir every few minutes. Turn off heat. Cover pan and let sit for 5–10 minutes until all the potatoes and ham are completely tender. Serve hot with your choice of vegetables. Top with additional cheese if desired.

*HAM is optional. If you make this meal without meat, reduce water to 4½ cups.

Estimated Shelf Life
if stored in a cool, dry place

5–10 YEARS

Jar ingredients:

2½ cups Honeyville dehydrated potato slices

½ cup Honeyville freeze-dried ham* (do not use TVP)

⅔ cup Honeyville all-purpose flour

¼ cup Honeyville powdered cheese sauce

½ cup Honeyville instant milk

2 Tbsp. Honeyville freeze-dried onion

2 Tbsp. Honeyville freeze-dried celery

½ cup Honeyville freeze-dried bell peppers

2 Tbsp. Honeyville powdered butter

1 tsp. Chef Tess All-Purpose seasoning

CHICKEN FRIED RICE

Jar ingredients:

½ cup Honeyville freeze-dried chicken

½ cup Honeyville freeze-dried scrambled eggs

1 cup Honeyville long-grain rice

1 cup Honeyville freeze-dried vegetable mix

¼ cup Honeyville freeze-dried onion

¼ cup Honeyville freeze-dried celery

¼ cup Honeyville freeze-dried bell peppers

¼ cup freeze-dried mushrooms

1 Tbsp. chicken bouillon

$\frac{1}{8}$ tsp. red pepper flakes

2 tsp. garlic granules

¼ tsp. hickory smoke powder*

½ cup soy sauce powder*

Fried rice can be full of added fat and calories, but this meal is made without extra fat and uses a lot of great vegetables!

Jar directions: Layer ingredients in a widemouthed quart-sized jar, shaking the dry powder ingredients into the bulkier items. Top with an oxygen packet for longer-term storage, cover with a new canning lid, and hand-tighten the metal ring.

Cooking directions: Bring 4½ cups of water to a rolling boil in a gallon-sized pot with a tight-fitting lid. Combine contents of the jar with the boiling water. Stir. Reduce heat to very low. Cover and simmer for 20–25 minutes until the rice is cooked and the vegetables are tender. Turn off heat and allow to sit, covered, for 5 minutes before serving. Serve hot.

*HICKORY SMOKE POWDER and SOY SAUCE POWDER are available online.

"BAKED" MACARONI ASPARAGUS AND CHEESE SKILLET CASSEROLE

This vegetarian meal is loaded with a creamy cheese sauce and plentiful chunks of asparagus! No baking required.

Estimated Shelf Life
if stored in a cool, dry place
10–15 YEARS

Jar directions: Layer jar ingredients in a widemouthed quart-sized jar, shaking the dry powder ingredients into the bulkier items. In a zip-sealable bag, add freeze-dried cheddar cheese. Squeeze air out of bag, zip seal, and place bag in jar. Top jar with an oxygen packet for longer-term storage, cover with a new canning lid, and hand-tighten the metal ring.

Cooking directions: Put contents of jar in a 12-inch skillet (with a lid). Add 5 cups of hot water. Bring to a boil and cover. Simmer 12–15 minutes until noodles are tender. Sauce will thicken a little more as it cools. Hydrate cheese by misting with a little cool water. Top macaroni with hydrated cheese and cover for 5 more minutes.

Jar ingredients:

¼ cup Honeyville cheese sauce powder

2 tsp. chicken bouillon

1 Tbsp. Honeyville freeze-dried onion

¼ cup Honeyville instant nonfat dry milk

½ cup Honeyville cream cheese powder

1 tsp. Chef Tess All-Purpose seasoning

1 cup Honeyville freeze-dried asparagus

1½ cup Honeyville elbow macaroni

Bag ingredients:

1 cup freeze-dried cheddar cheese

VEGGIE BARLEY AND BEAN CASSEROLE

Estimated
Shelf Life
if stored in a cool, dry place

10–15 YEARS

Jar ingredients:

1 cup Honeyville quick cook red beans

2 tsp. MSG-free chicken bouillon

1 cup Honeyville freeze-dried corn

¼ cup Honeyville dehydrated onion

¼ cup Honeyville freeze-dried bell peppers

½ cup Honeyville dehydrated celery

½ cup Honeyville pearled barley

½ cup Honeyville freeze-dried zucchini

¼ cup Honeyville tomato powder

2 tsp. Chef Tess All-Purpose seasoning

1 Tbsp. Honeyville lemonade powder

Jar directions: Layer ingredients in a widemouthed quart-sized jar, shaking the dry powder ingredients into the bulkier items. Top with an oxygen packet for longer-term storage, cover with a new canning lid, and hand-tighten the metal ring.

Cooking directions: Remove oxygen packet and discard. In a large saucepan, combine contents of the jar with 6½–7 cups of hot water and let simmer, covered, on low heat for 35–45 minutes until barley is tender.

YANKEE DOODLE MAC-N-CHEESE

This macaroni and cheese doesn't require any draining of the pasta or making of the sauce separately. It tastes like a baked casserole and is topped with a generous portion of real cheese!

Estimated Shelf Life
if stored in a cool, dry place
5–10 YEARS

Jar directions: Layer jar ingredients in a widemouthed quart-sized jar, shaking the dry powder ingredients into the bulkier items. In a zip-sealable bag, add freeze-dried cheddar cheese. Squeeze air out of the bag, twist closed, and place bag in jar. Top jar with an oxygen packet for longer-term storage, cover with a new canning lid, and hand-tighten the metal ring.

Cooking directions: Remove oxygen packet and discard. Put contents of jar in a 12-inch skillet (with a lid) Add 6 cups of hot water. Bring to a boil and cover. Simmer 12–15 minutes until noodles are tender. Sauce will thicken a little more as it cools. Hydrate cheese by misting it with a little cool water. Top macaroni with hydrated cheese and cover for 5 more minutes.

Jar ingredients:

- ¼ cup Honeyville cheese sauce powder
- 2 tsp. chicken bouillon
- 1 Tbsp. Honeyville freeze-dried onion
- ¼ cup instant nonfat dry milk
- ¼ cup Honeyville cream cheese powder
- ½ tsp. Chef Tess All-Purpose seasoning
- 2 cups elbow macaroni
- ¼ tsp. turmeric (for color)

Bag ingredients:

- 1 cup Honeyville freeze-dried cheddar cheese

Spicy Moroccan-Style
Butter Chicken with Basmati

SPICY MOROCCAN-STYLE
BUTTER CHICKEN WITH BASMATI

Basmati is an aromatic aged rice that is light and flavorful. It's the perfect companion to this Indian-style butter chicken.

Jar directions: Layer jar ingredients in a wide-mouth, quart-sized jar, shaking the dry powder ingredients into the bulkier items. In a zip-sealable bag, add bag ingredients. Squeeze air out of bag, zip seal, and place bag in jar. Top jar with an oxygen packet for longer-term storage, cover with a new canning lid, and hand-tighten the metal ring.

Cooking directions: Remove oxygen packet and discard. Combine contents of the jar with 5 cups of hot water in a large pot and let simmer for 15–20 minutes. In a separate covered saucepan, add 2¼ cups of water and bag ingredients. Simmer on low heat for 15–20 minutes. Remove cardamom pods before serving.

*CARDAMOM PODS are an Indian spice that can be found in most grocery store baking aisles. They lend a lemony and complex flavor to the rice.

Estimated Shelf Life
if stored in a cool, dry place
5–10 YEARS

Jar ingredients:

2 cups Honeyville freeze-dried chicken

⅔ cup Honeyville tomato powder

⅓ cup Honeyville powdered butter

⅓ cup Honeyville dehydrated onion

2 tsp. MSG-free chicken bouillon

¼ cup Honeyville dehydrated carrot

1 tsp. whole cumin seeds

2 tsp. garam masala blend

1 tsp. hot pepper flakes

½ cup Honeyville freeze-dried mangos

Bag ingredients:

1 cup basmati or Honeyville parboiled rice

½ tsp. whole cumin seeds

2 cardamom pods*

2 Tbsp. Honeyville powdered butter

½ tsp. salt

CHUNKY ITALIAN SPAGHETTI

Estimated
Shelf Life
if stored in a cool, dry place

7–10 YEARS

I have a boy who would eat spaghetti every single night and never get bored with it. He's a full-grown man, by the way, and I'm married to him. My husband is a kid at heart, but that doesn't mean he eats like one. This is a comforting spaghetti dinner that is sure to satisfy anyone.

Jar ingredients:

4 oz. spaghetti, broken to fit quart-sized jar

½ cup Honeyville freeze-dried mushroom

½ cup Honeyville freeze-dried sausage or sausage TVP

¼ cup Honeyville dehydrated carrots

⅓ cup Honeyville freeze-dried bell pepper

2 Tbsp. Honeyville dehydrated onion

⅔ cup Honeyville tomato powder

1 Tbsp. granulated honey

1 Tbsp. Chef Tess Romantic Italian Seasoning

Jar directions: Layer ingredients in a widemouthed quart-sized jar, shaking the dry powder ingredients into the bulkier items. Top with an oxygen packet for longer-term storage, cover with a new canning lid, and hand-tighten the metal ring.

Cooking directions: Remove oxygen packet and discard. In a 2-quart pot, bring 5½–6 cups of water to a rolling boil. Add contents of jar and stir well. Simmer over medium-high heat for 10–12 minutes until pasta and vegetables are tender. Stir occasionally. Add more water if you like your sauce more thin.

HAM AND HASH BROWNS O'BRIEN CASSEROLE

Potatoes with ham and aromatic vegetables make up the base of this creamy saucy casserole.

Jar directions: Layer ingredients in a widemouthed, quart-sized jar, shaking the dry powder ingredients into the bulkier items. Top with an oxygen packet for longer-term storage, cover with a new canning lid, and hand-tighten the metal ring.

Cooking directions: Remove oxygen packet and discard. Combine ingredients in a deep casserole dish with 6 cups of hot water. Cover for 10 minutes. Bake covered in a preheated oven at 350°F for 1 hour or in the microwave uncovered on high for 15 minutes.

Estimated Shelf Life
if stored in a cool, dry place
5–10 YEARS

Jar ingredients:

1 cup Honeyville freeze-dried ham

1½ cups Honeyville dehydrated hash brown potatoes

½ cup Honeyville freeze-dried bell peppers

½ cup Honeyville dehydrated shoestring carrots

¾ cup Honeyville powdered cheese sauce

1 cup Honeyville sour cream powder or cream cheese powder

⅓ cup Honeyville dehydrated onion

1½ tsp. dehydrated minced garlic

CLASSIC SPANISH PAELLA

Jar ingredients:

2 Tbsp. powdered butter

½ cup Honeyville
freeze-dried sausage

1 Tbsp. chorizo seasoning*

¼ cup Honeyville
dehydrated onion

1 Tbsp. granulated garlic

¼ cup Honeyville tomato
powder

1 cup parboiled rice

2 Tbsp. burgundy wine
powder** (optional)

1 tsp. Spanish saffron

½ cup Honeyville
freeze-dried mushroom

½ cup Honeyville
freeze-dried peas

1 cup Honeyville
freeze-dried chicken

2 tsp. Kikkoman seafood
soup mix, scallop flavor***
(contains MSG)

1 Tbsp. Honeyville
dehydrated parsley

Traditional Spanish paella with chorizo, chicken, and seafood is quite popular. In this dish, we're leaving out the fish and using mushrooms like they do in the interior of Spain.

Jar directions: Layer ingredients in a wide-mouth, quart-sized jar, shaking the dry powder ingredients into the bulkier items. Top with an oxygen packet for longer-term storage, cover with a new canning lid, and hand-tighten the metal ring.

Cooking directions: Remove oxygen packet and discard. In a 4-quart pot with a tight-fitting lid, add 4½ cups of hot water and contents of jar. Bring to a boil and then reduce to low heat and cover. Simmer for 20–25 minutes. Serve hot.

*CHORIZO SEASONING can be found at many Mexican markets and grocery stores.

**BURGUNDY WINE POWDER is available at Honeyville retail stores.

***SEAFOOD SOUP MIX can be found at Asian markets.

Estimated
Shelf Life
if stored in a cool, dry place

5–10
YEARS

Classic Spanish Paella

GRANDMA'S CHICKEN AND RICE SKILLET CASSEROLE

Jar ingredients:

¼ cup flour

2 tsp. chicken bouillon

2 Tbsp. French onion soup mix

¼ cup Honeyville instant nonfat dry milk

½ cup Honeyville cream cheese powder

½ tsp. Chef Tess All-Purpose seasoning

½ cup Honeyville freeze-dried mushroom slices

¼ cup Honeyville freeze-dried celery

½ tsp. Chef Tess The Big Dill seasoning

1½ cup Honeyville freeze-dried chicken

1½ cups Honeyville long-grain rice

3 Tbsp. vinegar powder

½ tsp. baking soda

For years on Sundays, my mother would put a chicken and rice casserole in the slow cooker before we left for services. She is now the grandmother to my children and still enjoys cooking with love in mind. This is a mild, creamy comfort food. I'll always think of my mom when I eat this dish, which I converted from her original recipe.

Jar directions: Layer ingredients in a widemouthed quart-sized jar, shaking the dry powder ingredients into the bulkier items. Top with an oxygen packet for longer-term storage, cover with a new canning lid, and hand-tighten the metal ring.

Cooking directions: Remove oxygen packet and discard. Combine contents of the jar with 6 cups of hot water in a large covered pot and let simmer on very low heat for 15–20 minutes. Allow to sit for 5 minutes off the heat before serving. Sauce will thicken slightly.

Estimated Shelf Life
if stored in a cool, dry place
5–10 YEARS

CHEF TESS'S VEGETARIAN BASE

This is a vegetarian base recipe, which is used in the next 3 recipes. Begin with this base recipe in your jar and then finish it with a recipe that corresponds. From these humble beginnings, you can add a number of different sauces that change the whole flavor profile of this basic vegetarian base. But be sure to weigh the noodles and not just guess. If the noodles are long, break them into smaller pieces to fit into the jars.

Estimated Shelf Life
if stored in a cool, dry place
10–15 YEARS

Jar ingredients:

4 oz. spaghetti noodles

¼ cup Honeyville dehydrated carrots

⅓ cup Honeyville freeze-dried peas

⅓ cup Honeyville freeze-dried bell pepper

1 scant cup Honeyville freeze-dried mushrooms

1 cup Honeyville freeze-dried zucchini

2 Tbsp. Honeyville freeze-dried onion

Jar directions: Layer ingredients in a widemouthed quart-sized jar, shaking the dry powder ingredients into the bulkier items. Add additional ingredients from other recipes that use this base recipe to create the recipe of your choice. Top with an oxygen packet for longer-term storage, cover with a new canning lid, and hand-tighten the metal ring.

Cooking directions: Follow the directions given for one of the following 3 recipes.

ITALIAN MARINARA AND SAUCY VEGETABLES (WITH VEGETARIAN BASE)

Estimated
Shelf Life
if stored in a cool, dry place

10–15 YEARS

Jar ingredients:

Add the following to Chef Tess's Vegetarian Base (p. 55):

⅔ cup Honeyville tomato powder

1 Tbsp. sugar or Honeyville granulated honey

1 Tbsp. Chef Tess's Romantic Italian seasoning

Jar directions: Layer ingredients in a widemouthed quart-sized jar, shaking the dry powder ingredients into the bulkier items. Top with an oxygen packet for longer-term storage, cover with a new canning lid, and hand-tighten the metal ring.

Cooking directions: Remove oxygen packet and discard. In a 2-quart pot, bring 5 cups of water to a rolling boil. Pour contents of jar into boiling water and stir. Boil for 8–10 minutes until noodles are tender. Serve hot.

CLASSIC CREAMY PASTA PRIMAVERA (WITH VEGETARIAN BASE)

Jar directions: Layer ingredients in a widemouthed quart-sized jar, shaking the dry powder ingredients into the bulkier items. Top with an oxygen packet for longer-term storage, cover with a new canning lid, and hand-tighten the metal ring.

Estimated Shelf Life
if stored in a cool, dry place
10–15 YEARS

Cooking directions: Remove oxygen packet and discard. In a 2-quart pot, bring 4½ cups of water to a rolling boil. Pour contents of jar into boiling water and stir. Boil for 8–10 minutes until noodles are tender. Serve hot.

*NOTE: ¼ cup regular cornstarch can be used in place of ultra gel, but be sure to bring to a boil when cooking.

Jar ingredients:

Add the following to Chef Tess's Vegetarian Base (p. 55):

⅓ cup ultra gel* (modified cornstarch)

1 Tbsp. MSG-free chicken bouillon

¼ cup Honeyville instant milk

¼ cup Honeyville sour cream powder

1 Tbsp. Chef Tess Romantic Italian seasoning

Oriental Ginger Noodle Wok

ORIENTAL GINGER NOODLE
WOK (WITH VEGETARIAN BASE)

Jar directions: Layer ingredients in a widemouthed quart-sized jar, shaking the dry powder ingredients into the bulkier items. Top with an oxygen packet for longer-term storage, cover with a new canning lid, and hand-tighten the metal ring.

Estimated Shelf Life
if stored in a cool, dry place
10–15 YEARS

Cooking directions: Remove oxygen packet and discard. In a 2-quart pot, bring 4½ cups of water to a rolling boil. Pour contents of jar into boiling water and stir. Boil for 8–10 minutes until noodles are tender. Cool for 5 minutes and allow to thicken slightly. Serve hot.

*NOTE: ¼ cup regular cornstarch can be used in place of ultra gel, but be sure to bring to a boil when cooking.

Jar ingredients:

Add the following to Chef Tess's Vegetarian Base (p. 55):

¼ cup ultra gel*
(modified cornstarch)

1 Tbsp. MSG-free chicken bouillon (optional)

1 tsp. red pepper flakes (optional)

1 Tbsp. garlic powder

1 Tbsp. Chef Tess Amazing Wok-Star seasoning (not gluten-free)

2 Tbsp. Honeyville granulated honey

2 Tbsp. vinegar powder

¼ tsp. hickory smoke powder

VEGAN SWEET POTATO DAHL

Estimated Shelf Life
if stored in a cool, dry place

10–15 YEARS

There are thousands of variations of dahl, a thick Indian stew generally served with hot rice or flat bread. This is our family's favorite. Red lentils cook slightly faster than others, and they cook into a creamy-textured hearty dish.

Jar ingredients:

1 cup Honeyville freeze-dried sweet potato

⅓ cup Honeyville freeze-dried onion

½ tsp. dehydrated minced garlic

½ tsp. red pepper flakes

1 tsp. Chef Tess Gingham Masala*

½ tsp. mustard seed

½ cup red lentils

Bag ingredients:

2 cups basmati rice or Honeyville long-grain rice

2 cardamom pod

½ tsp. cumin seed

¼ tsp. salt

pinch of red pepper flakes

Jar directions: Layer ingredients in a widemouthed, quart-sized jar, shaking the dry powder ingredients into the bulkier items. In a zip-sealable bag, add bag ingredients. Squeeze air out of bag, twist closed, and place bag in jar. Top jar with an oxygen packet for longer-term storage, cover with a new canning lid, and hand-tighten the metal ring.

Cooking directions: Remove oxygen packet and discard. In a 2-quart pot, add 4½–5 cups of water and add jar ingredients. Simmer on low heat for 35–45 minutes until desired thickness. In a separate 2-quart pot, empty the bag ingredients into 3¾ cups of water and simmer covered on low heat for 20 minutes. Serve the dahl over the cooked rice.

*GINGHAM MASALA is a specialty blend of spices similar in flavor to tandoori masala. I made it to benefit impoverished HIV orphan children. We do this through education and providing healthy meals in India through the help of ginghamproject.org. This particular blend can be ordered online.

Vegan Sweet Potato Dahl

ROMANTIC ITALIAN CHICKEN CACCIATORE WITH BEANS

Estimated
Shelf Life
if stored in a cool, dry place

5–10 YEARS

Jar ingredients:

¼ cup Honeyville dehydrated onion

¼ cup Honeyville dehydrated carrot

2 Tbsp. Honeyville dehydrated celery

1½ tsp. dehydrated minced garlic

1 cup Honeyville freeze-dried white chicken

½ tsp. salt

½ tsp. black pepper

½ cup Honeyville tomato powder

2 tsp. MSG-free chicken bouillon

2 tsp. Romantic Italian seasoning

2 cups Honeyville quick-cook red beans

Break out the wax drippy candles, red checkerboard tablecloths, and some crusty Italian garlic bread—this delightful meal is just as good as sitting down in a restaurant!

Jar directions: Layer ingredients in a widemouthed quart-sized jar, shaking the dry powder ingredients into the bulkier items. Top with an oxygen packet for longer-term storage, cover with a new canning lid, and hand-tighten the metal ring.

Cooking directions: Remove oxygen packet and discard. Combine contents of the jar with 6 cups of hot water in a large pot and let simmer for 15–20 minutes.

APRICOT CHICKEN BARLEY PILAF

As a restaurant chef, I would always serve dried apricot and rosemary rolled inside a chicken cutlet. I fell in love with that flavor combination and quickly converted it to a jar meal mixed into a hearty barley pilaf.

Estimated Shelf Life
if stored in a cool, dry place

10–15 YEARS

J ar directions: Layer ingredients in a widemouthed quart-sized jar, shaking the dry powder ingredients into the bulkier items. Top with an oxygen packet for longer-term storage, cover with a new canning lid, and hand-tighten the metal ring.

C ooking directions: Remove oxygen packet and discard. Combine contents of the jar with 6 cups of hot water in a large covered pot and let simmer on low heat for 35–45 minutes.

Jar ingredients:

1 cup Honeyville pearled barley

1 cup Honeyville freeze-dried chicken

1 Tbsp. MSG-free chicken bouillon

1 tsp. fennel seed

2 tsp. dried rosemary

2 tsp. Chef Tess French Provencal Essential seasoning

½ cup Honeyville freeze-dried apricots

⅓ cup Honeyville dehydrated onion

2 tsp. granulated garlic

Spicy Chicken in Peanut
Sauce Over Rice

SPICY CHICKEN IN PEANUT SAUCE OVER RICE

If I had a dollar for how many times people said, "Wow!" when eating this meal, I'd have a lot of dollars. You control how spicy your peanut sauce is, so it is never too hot for kids.

Jar directions: Layer ingredients in a widemouthed quart-sized jar, shaking the dry powder ingredients into the bulkier items. In a zip-sealable bag, add bag ingredients. Squeeze air out of bag, zip seal, and place bag in jar. Top jar with an oxygen packet for longer-term storage, cover with a new canning lid, and hand-tighten the metal ring.

Cooking directions: In a 2-quart pot with a lid, combine the rice in the bag with 3 cups of hot water. Cover tightly and simmer on very low heat for 20 minutes. While the rice is cooking, combine the jar contents with 3 cups of water and simmer on low heat for 15–20 minutes until vegetables and meat are hydrated and sauce thickens slightly.

Estimated Shelf Life
if stored in a cool, dry place
5–10 YEARS

Jar ingredients:

1½ cup Honeyville freeze-dried chicken

½ cup soy sauce powder

2 Tbsp. Honeyville lemonade powder

1 Tbsp. dehydrated garlic slices

⅓ cup Honeyville powdered peanut butter

1 tsp. red pepper flakes (more or less depending on how hot you like your meals)

⅓ cup Honeyville dehydrated onion

⅔ Honeyville dehydrated carrot

1 Tbsp. dry cilantro

1 Tbsp. ultra gel (or 2 Tbsp. cornstarch)

Bag ingredient:

1½ cups long-grain rice

CHINESE STICKY RICE

Estimated
Shelf Life
if stored in a cool, dry place

10–15
YEARS

I get the short-grain rice for this meal from a specialty oriental market, but you can use long-grain rice instead. This meal can be used as a main course or a side dish, but remember, it is filling! A little goes a long way.

Jar ingredients:

2 cups short-grain rice (sweet or glutinous)

½ cup Honeyville freeze-dried mushrooms

1 tsp. dehydrated minced garlic

½ cup Honeyville freeze-dried sausage

2 tsp. chicken bouillon

1 Tbsp. Chef Tess Amazing Wok-Star seasoning (or Chinese five-spice)

½ cup soy sauce powder*

¼ cup sherry wine powder (optional)*

½ tsp. hickory smoke powder*

½ cup Honeyville freeze-dried peas

½ cup Honeyville dehydrated green onion

Jar directions: Layer ingredients in a widemouthed quart-sized jar, shaking the dry powder ingredients into the bulkier items. Top with an oxygen packet for longer-term storage, cover with a new canning lid, and hand-tighten the metal ring.

Cooking directions: Remove oxygen packet and discard. In a 2-quart pot, combine contents of the jar with 5½ cups of water. Simmer covered on low heat for 30–35 minutes.

*THESE ITEMS are available online.

STEWS AND SOUPS

CHEF TESS'S CONDENSED CREAM SOUP

Jar ingredients:

¼ cup ultra gel*
  (modified cornstarch)

2 tsp. MSG-free chicken
  bouillon

1 Tbsp. Honeyville
  freeze-dried onions

¼ cup Honeyville instant
  milk

2 Tbsp. Honeyville sour
  cream powder

½ tsp. Chef Tess All-Purpose
  seasoning

Variation for cream of mushroom:

¼ cup Honeyville
  freeze-dried mushrooms
  (crush down to 2 Tbsp.)

Variation for cream of celery:

2 Tbsp. Honeyville
  freeze-dried celery

How many recipes do you have that start with a can of condensed cream soup? How about cutting that expense from your family food budget and making your own? It's easy, delicious, and budget friendly! I've even included my variations to create mushroom or celery cream soup. This recipe makes the equivalent of one regular-sized can of condensed cream soup. If you put one batch of jar ingredients into a snack-sized, zip-seal bag, you can fit up to four baggies in one widemouthed quart-sized jar. I don't even write cooking directions on each baggy—I write how much water to add for one baggy on the top of the jar.

Jar directions: Layer ingredients into a snack-sized, zip-seal baggy. Expel as much air out as possible when sealing. Stuff up to four baggies into a widemouthed quart-sized jar. Top jar with an oxygen packet for longer-term storage, cover with a new canning lid, and hand-tighten the metal ring.

Cooking directions: Empty the contents of one snack baggy into a pot with 1¼ cups of water. Whisk over medium heat for about 5 minutes until thick. It will thicken more as it cools, so don't add extra thickener or you'll end up with glue. Use this as a straight-across substitute in any recipe that calls for a can of condensed cream soup!

*NOTE: ¼ cup regular cornstarch can be used in place of the ultra gel, but be sure to bring to a boil when cooking.

Estimated
Shelf Life
if stored in a cool, dry place

5–10
YEARS

Chef Tess's Condensed
Cream Soup Mix

COUNTRY-STYLE HAMBURGER STEW

Estimated
Shelf Life
if stored in a cool, dry place **10–15 YEARS**

This is an amazing recipe for camping or dinner any night of the week. It's perfect for giving to a sick neighbor. I think my family appreciates it because the folks I tend to cook for are down-home, raised-on-the-farm kind of people. Serve this with your favorite country biscuits.

Jar ingredients:

1 cup Honeyville quick-cook red beans

1 cup Honeyville freeze-dried mixed vegetables

1 cup Honeyville freeze-dried ground beef (or TVP beef)

1 cup Honeyville dehydrated diced potatoes

¼ cup Honeyville dehydrated onions

¼ cup Honeyville tomato powder

1 tsp. thyme

1 tsp. granulated garlic

¼ cup flour (or 2 Tbsp. cornstarch)

1 Tbsp. MSG-free beef bouillon

Jar directions: Layer ingredients in a widemouthed quart-sized jar, shaking the dry powder ingredients into the bulkier items. It will fit if you shake it really well. Top with an oxygen packet for longer-term storage, cover with a new canning lid, and hand-tighten the metal ring.

Cooking directions: Remove oxygen packet and discard. In a 4-quart pot, combine stew mix with 6 cups of water and bring to a boil. Reduce the heat and simmer for 20–30 minutes.

TACO SOUP

This recipe is adapted from an old classic and uses instant beans. Instead of taking hours to cook in a slow cooker, it takes about 20 minutes!

Estimated Shelf Life
if stored in a cool, dry place

10–15 YEARS

Jar directions: Layer ingredients in a widemouthed quart-sized jar, shaking the dry powder ingredients into the bulkier items. Top with an oxygen packet for longer-term storage, cover with a new canning lid, and hand-tighten the metal ring.

Cooking directions: Remove oxygen packet and discard. Place contents of jar in a 4-quart pot. Add 8 cups of water and simmer for 20–30 minutes until veggies are tender. Serve with tortilla chips, sour cream, and salsa if desired.

Jar ingredients:

1½ cups Honeyville quick-cook red or black beans

1 cup Honeyville taco-flavored TVP

½ cup Honeyville dehydrated onion

⅓ cup Honeyville freeze-dried mixed peppers

¾ cup Honeyville freeze-dried corn

½ cup Honeyville tomato powder

1 Tbsp. Chef Tess Southwest Fajita seasoning or homemade taco seasoning

Dallas-Style Chicken
Noodle Soup

DALLAS-STYLE CHICKEN NOODLE SOUP

This meal was a request from a friend named Dallas at the Honeyville store in Arizona. It has nothing to do with anything actually in Dallas, Texas. Sorry, Texas. As for Dallas, she loves chicken noodle soup but, as she put it, "without all the vegetables and big herbs and stuff in there." I love her and she's a great reminder that, though I may be creating some remarkable gourmet Meals in a Jar that span international cuisine, there's also a need for some basic meals every family in the good ol' United States of America will eat. This meal is made in a pint-size jar, so make sure you have the smaller jars on hand.

Jar directions: Layer ingredients in a widemouthed pint-sized jar, shaking the dry powder ingredients into the bulkier items. Top with an oxygen packet for longer-term storage, cover with a new canning lid, and hand-tighten the metal ring.

Cooking directions: Remove oxygen packet and discard. Empty contents of the jar into 5 cups of boiling water in a half-gallon pot. Simmer for 12–15 minutes until chicken and noodles are tender. Serve hot.

Estimated Shelf Life
if stored in a cool, dry place
10 YEARS

Jar ingredients:

(Use a pint-sized jar)

½ cup Honeyville freeze-dried white chicken or chicken-flavored TVP

1½ cups broken linguine or fettuccine noodles (I go by weight—3.5 oz.)

1 Tbsp. plus 1 tsp. MSG-free chicken bouillon

1 tsp. garlic granules or powder

¼ tsp. dry thyme

¼ tsp. Chef Tess All-Purpose seasoning

⅛ tsp. turmeric (for color and flavor)

CHEF TESS'S CLASSIC CHILI

Estimated
Shelf Life
if stored in a cool, dry place

10 YEARS

This is a classic chili. Some like it hot. Some like it mild. But 99 percent of the people I know will eat it at least twice a month . . . if not more.

Jar ingredients:

- 2 cups Honeyville quick-cook red or black beans
- 1 cup Honeyville tomato powder
- 1 cup Honeyville freeze-dried diced beef or chili TVP
- ½ cup Honeyville dehydrated onion
- ½ cup Honeyville freeze-dried bell peppers
- ¼ cup Honeyville freeze-dried celery
- 1 Tbsp. MSG-free beef bouillon
- 1 Tbsp. chili powder (more or less, depending on how you like your chili)
- 1 Tbsp. Chef Tess All-Purpose seasoning
- 1 tsp. hot chili flakes (optional; if you like it hot)

Jar directions: Layer ingredients in a widemouthed quart-sized jar, shaking the dry powder ingredients into the bulkier items. Pack the ingredients as tightly as possible. Top with an oxygen packet for longer-term storage, cover with a new canning lid, and hand-tighten the metal ring.

Cooking directions: Remove oxygen packet and discard. Empty the contents of the jar into a gallon-sized pot with 7–8 cups of hot water (depending on how thick you like your chili). Simmer over medium-high heat for 25–30 minutes until rehydrated and ready to eat. Serve with hydrated, freeze-dried cheese if desired or just have it plain in all its glory.

POTATO, HAM, AND MUSHROOM CHOWDER

Jar directions: Layer ingredients in a widemouthed quart-sized jar, shaking the dry powder ingredients into the bulkier items. Top with an oxygen packet for longer-term storage, cover with a new canning lid, and hand-tighten the metal ring.

Cooking directions: Remove oxygen packet and discard. In a large pot, combine contents of the jar with 10 cups of cool water and bring to a boil. Reduce heat and simmer for 15–20 minutes, stirring occasionally.

Estimated Shelf Life
if stored in a cool, dry place
5–10 YEARS

Jar ingredients:

1 cup Honeyville freeze-dried ham

1 cup Honeyville freeze-dried mushrooms

3 cups Honeyville creamy potato soup mix

1 bay leaf

2 tsp. Chef Tess The Big Dill seasoning

FRENCH HAM CASSOULET

Jar ingredients:

- 2 cups Honeyville quick-cook red beans or make your own quick-cook white beans*

- 1 cup Honeyville freeze-dried ham

- ½ cup Honeyville freeze-dried sausage

- ½ cup Honeyville tomato powder

- ¼ cup Honeyville freeze-dried or dehydrated onion

- ¼ cup Honeyville dehydrated carrots

- ¼ cup Honeyville dehydrated celery

- 2 tsp. Chef Tess French Provencal Essential seasoning

- ¼ cup powdered butter

- 1 Tbsp. dehydrated minced garlic

- 3 Tbsp. sherry or burgundy wine powder** (optional)

- 1 bay leaf

Jar directions: Layer ingredients in a widemouthed, quart-sized jar, shaking the dry powder ingredients into the bulkier items. Top with an oxygen packet for longer-term storage, cover with a new canning lid, and hand-tighten the metal ring.

Cooking directions: Remove oxygen packet and discard.

STOVETOP: Empty contents of jar into a 4-quart covered pot with 7 cups of water. Simmer for 15–20 minutes until beans are tender.

TRADITIONAL OVEN: Bake in a gallon-sized shallow earthenware pot, covered, for 1 hour at 350°F until thick.

*TRADITIONALLY, ham cassoulet is made with white beans. Honeyville sells the most amazing navy beans. If you have an abundance of navy beans and would like to make your own quick-cook white beans, simply place cooked, rinsed beans that have been patted dry in your food dehydrator on the "jerky" setting. Dry until completely crisp. Use them here, and they'll be shelf stable for your long-term storage and be ready to eat in 20 minutes of cooking!

**BURGUNDY WINE POWDER is available at Honeyville stores. If it is not available, omit from recipe.

Estimated Shelf Life
if stored in a cool, dry place
10–15 YEARS

French Ham Cassoulet

Sweet Potato
and Chicken Stew

SWEET POTATO AND CHICKEN STEW

A unique combination of Indian spices and sweet potato gives this hearty tomato-based stew a satisfying flavor. The first time I tasted it, it became one of my favorites!

Jar directions: Layer ingredients in a widemouthed quart-sized jar, shaking the dry powder ingredients into the bulkier items. Top with an oxygen packet for longer-term storage, cover with a new canning lid, and hand-tighten the metal ring.

Cooking directions: Remove oxygen packet and discard. Add 8 cups of water to the jar ingredients in a saucepan and simmer over low heat for 15–20 minutes.

*GINGHAM MASALA is a specialty blend of spices similar in flavor to tandoori masala. I made it to benefit impoverished HIV orphan children. We do this through education and providing healthy meals in India through the help of ginghamproject.org. This particular blend can be ordered online.

**GRANULATED BELL PEPPER can be replaced with ground bell pepper by pulsing the freeze-dried peppers in a blender for 5–10 seconds.

Jar ingredients:

½ cup Honeyville dehydrated onion

2 Tbsp. dehydrated minced garlic

2 tsp. Chef Tess Gingham Masala*

½ cup Honeyville freeze-dried celery

½ cup Honeyville dehydrated carrot

¼ cup red bell pepper granules**

1 cup Honeyville freeze-dried sweet potatoes

1 Tbsp. MSG-free chicken bouillon

1 cup Honeyville freeze-dried chicken

½ cup Honeyville powdered peanut butter

2 Tbsp. dehydrated cilantro

1⅓ cup Honeyville tomato powder

Estimated Shelf Life
if stored in a cool, dry place
7–10 YEARS

CLASSIC YANKEE CHICKEN BAKED BEANS

Estimated
Shelf Life
if stored in a cool, dry place

**10–15
YEARS**

Jar ingredients:

2½ cups quick-cook red
beans

¼ cup Honeyville
dehydrated onion

¼ cup Honeyville tomato
powder

½ cup Honeyville granulated
honey

2 Tbsp. mustard powder*

2 Tbsp. vinegar powder**

1 cup Honeyville
freeze-dried chicken

1 tsp. maple flavor
powder*** (optional)

1 tsp. Chef Tess All-Purpose
seasoning

Jar directions: Layer ingredients in a widemouthed quart-sized jar, shaking the dry powder ingredients into the bulkier items. Top with an oxygen packet for longer-term storage, cover with a new canning lid, and hand-tighten the metal ring.

Cooking directions: Remove oxygen packet and discard. Empty jar ingredients into a saucepan. Add 6 cups of water. Simmer over low heat for 20–25 minutes or bake uncovered at 350°F for 35–40 minutes.

*MUSTARD POWDER is not ground mustard seed—it is a dry "prepared mustard." Firehousepantrystore.com carries it.

**VINEGAR POWDER can be found at Honeyville retail locations and online.

***MAPLE FLAVOR POWDER can be found at Honeyville retail locations and is sometimes available in health food stores or grocery store baking aisles by the frosting flavorings.

FRENCH CREAM OF ASPARAGUS SOUP WITH HAM

Jar directions: Layer ingredients in a widemouthed quart-sized jar, shaking the dry powder ingredients into the bulkier items. Top with an oxygen packet for longer-term storage, cover with a new canning lid, and hand-tighten the metal ring.

Estimated
Shelf Life
if stored in a cool, dry place

5–10 YEARS

Cooking directions: In a pot, bring 5½ cups of water to a boil. Add jar ingredients. Reduce heat and simmer on low heat for 10–15 minutes until meat and vegetables are tender and soup is slightly thickened. Cover and turn off heat. Allow to sit 5 minutes. Serve hot.

Jar ingredients:

1 cup Honeyville freeze-dried ham

1 cup Honeyville freeze-dried corn

¼ cup Honeyville freeze-dried onion

¼ cup Honeyville freeze-dried celery

¼ cup Honeyville freeze-dried asparagus

½ cup Honeyville instant dry milk powder

½ cup Honeyville sour cream powder

½ cup Honeyville dehydrated diced potatoes

¼ cup Honeyville cheese sauce powder

1½ tsp. Chef Tess French Provencal Essential seasoning

BRAZILIAN RUSTIC CHICKEN VATAPA

Estimated
Shelf Life
if stored in a cool, dry place

**5–10
YEARS**

This is an amazingly adaptable stew from Bahia, Brazil, which is known for its dynamic cuisine. Often, bread is used as the thickener for this stew. The addition of coconut provides signature floral notes to the dish that are quite distinct.

Jar ingredients:

- ¼ cup Honeyville dehydrated onion
- 1 Tbsp. dehydrated minced garlic
- 1 Tbsp. dehydrated jalapeño (less if you want a milder flavor)
- ½ cup Honeyville tomato powder
- ¼ cup Honeyville peanut butter powder
- 1½ cup Honeyville freeze-dried chicken
- 2 tsp. coconut powder flavor
- 2 Tbsp. spray-dried beer powder* (optional)
- ½ cup Honeyville nonfat dry milk powder
- 1 tsp. baking soda

Jar directions: Layer ingredients in a widemouthed quart-sized jar, shaking the dry powder ingredients into the bulkier items. Top with an oxygen packet for longer-term storage, cover with a new canning lid, and hand-tighten the metal ring.

Cooking directions: Remove oxygen packet and discard. Combine contents of the jar with 4½ cups of cool water in a large pot and bring to a boil. Reduce heat and simmer for 15–20 minutes, stirring occasionally.

*SPRAY-DRIED BEER POWDER is a non-alcoholic powder flavoring used to add depth to the dish. It is available online.

Brazilian Rustic Chicken Vatapa

BLACK BEAN AND CHORIZO CHILI

Estimated
Shelf Life
if stored in a cool, dry place

10–15 YEARS

Jar ingredients:

2 Tbsp. ground pasilla chili
pepper

2 tsp. smoked paprika

½ cup Honeyville
dehydrated onion

½ cup Honeyville
freeze-dried bell pepper

1 cup Honeyville
freeze-dried sausage

2 tsp. cumin seeds

1 Tbsp. Mexican oregano
leaves

¼ tsp. Chef Tess Wise
Woman of the East spice
blend

2 Tbsp. lime juice powder

2 cups Honeyville quick-cook
black beans

1 Tbsp. Honeyville baker's
cocoa

This is a really unique chili with some southwestern flair. The addition of cocoa adds a deep flavor to the dish.

Jar directions: Layer ingredients in a widemouthed quart-sized jar, shaking the dry powder ingredients into the bulkier items. Top with an oxygen packet for longer-term storage, cover with a new canning lid, and hand-tighten the metal ring.

Cooking directions: Remove oxygen packet and discard. In a saucepan, combine jar ingredients with 6 cups of water and simmer for 20 minutes until beans are tender.

PAPAS CON CARNE STEW

Jar directions: Layer ingredients in a widemouthed quart-sized jar, shaking the dry powder ingredients into the bulkier items. Top with an oxygen packet for longer-term storage, cover with a new canning lid, and hand-tighten the metal ring.

Estimated Shelf Life
if stored in a cool, dry place
10–15 YEARS

Cooking directions: Remove oxygen packet and discard. In a saucepan, combine jar ingredients with 6–7 cups of water and simmer until potatoes and beef are tender, about 20 minutes.

Jar ingredients:

1 cup Honeyville freeze-dried beef dices

½ cup Honeyville dehydrated onion

½ cup Honeyville freeze-dried bell pepper

1 Tbsp. Chef Tess Southwest Fajita seasoning

2 cups Honeyville dehydrated diced potatoes

2 Tbsp. vinegar powder

1 Tbsp. paprika

1 Tbsp. granulated garlic

1 Tbsp. bouillon powder

Creamy Potato Cheese and Ham Soup

CREAMY POTATO CHEESE AND HAM SOUP

This meal makes a hearty and filling creamy soup. It is perfect on a cold winter's night.

Jar directions: Layer ingredients in a wide-mouth, quart-sized jar, shaking the dry powder ingredients into the bulkier items. Top with an oxygen packet for longer-term storage, cover with a new canning lid, and hand-tighten the metal ring.

Cooking directions: Remove oxygen packet and discard. Combine contents of the jar with 10 cups of cool water in a large pot and bring to a boil. Reduce heat and simmer for 15–20 minutes, stirring occasionally.

Estimated Shelf Life *if stored in a cool, dry place* — 5–10 YEARS

Jar ingredients:

3 cups Honeyville creamy potato cheese soup mix

1 cup Honeyville freeze-dried ham (do not use the ham TVP for this)

1 bay leaf

1 tsp. dehydrated rosemary

½ tsp. cracked black pepper

CHEF TESS'S CREAMY TOMATO SOUP

Estimated Shelf Life *if stored in a cool, dry place* **5–10 YEARS**

Jar ingredients:

½ cup ultra gel*
(modified cornstarch)

1½ cups Honeyville nonfat
milk powder

½ cup Honeyville tomato
powder

1 bay leaf

1 Tbsp. Honeyville
dehydrated onion

¼ tsp. celery seed

2 tsp. granulated garlic

2 tsp. salt

1 tsp. baking soda

2 tsp. pepper

2 tsp. thyme

2 Tbsp. MSG-free bouillon
(optional; omit previous
salt if you use bullion)

The baking soda in this recipe will keep the milk from curdling in your pan when mixed with the tomato. It's magic!

Jar directions: Layer ingredients in a widemouthed quart-sized jar, shaking the dry powder ingredients into the bulkier items. Top with an oxygen packet for longer-term storage, cover with a new canning lid, and hand-tighten the metal ring.

Cooking directions: Remove oxygen packet and discard. In a large pot, combine contents of the jar with 6 cups of water. For a richer cream soup, use milk in place of the water. Whisk over medium heat until combined. Simmer for 15–20 minutes.

*NOTE: ⅓ cup regular cornstarch can be used in place of the ultra gel, but be sure to bring to a boil when cooking.

VIRGINIA BRUNSWICK STEW

I fell in love with this stew the first time I tasted it, on a cold wintery night. It is meaty and full of potatoes and corn with just a hint of smokiness. It's the perfect companion to some fluffy buttermilk biscuits or savory onion-dill dinner rolls.

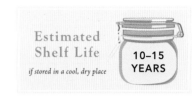

Estimated Shelf Life *if stored in a cool, dry place* — 10–15 YEARS

Jar directions: Layer ingredients in a widemouthed quart-sized jar, shaking the dry powder ingredients into the bulkier items. Top with an oxygen packet for longer-term storage, cover with a new canning lid, and hand-tighten the metal ring.

Cooking directions: Remove oxygen packet and discard. Empty contents of jar into a 4-quart pot and simmer with 5½ cups of water for 20–25 minutes.

Jar ingredients:

1 cup Honeyville dehydrated diced potato

½ cup Honeyville dehydrated onion

1 cup Honeyville freeze-dried corn

½ cup quick-cook white beans (make your own) or Honeyville quick-cook red beans

1 cup Honeyville freeze-dried chicken

½ tsp. smoked paprika or ¼ tsp. hickory smoke powder

1 tsp. Chef Tess All-Purpose seasoning

1 Tbsp. bouillon powder (optional)

ODE TO D'ATRI'S MINESTRONE

Jar ingredients:

¼ cup Honeyville
freeze-dried onion

1 cup Honeyville
freeze-dried zucchini

¼ cup Honeyville
dehydrated carrot

¼ cup Honeyville
freeze-dried celery

½ cup Honeyville tomato
powder

¼ cup Honeyville
freeze-dried spinach

½ cup Honeyville quick-cook
red beans

1 Tbsp. vegetarian bouillon
(optional)

1 Tbsp. Chef Tess Romantic
Italian seasoning

1 Tbsp. dehydrated basil
flakes

½ cup Honeyville
dehydrated diced potato

½ tsp. red pepper flakes

1 tsp. garlic powder

Bag ingredient:

½ cup Honeyville elbow
macaroni

D'Atri's Italian Restaurant was a popular and remarkable location run by the famous D'Atri family during the 1950s and '60s. It was the hallmark of fine dining at Lake Tahoe and the gathering spot of celebrities during that era. That being said, over the last year I've had the chance to be on a weekly radio show in Phoenix with Jan and Momma D'Atri. They are both elegant and charming women with true heart. It has been a real honor. I converted this recipe from the original minestrone recipe that they shared with me. It's not exactly their recipe, but it is pretty close! Thank you, my darling ladies!

Jar directions: Layer ingredients in a widemouthed, quart-sized jar, shaking the dry powder ingredients into the bulkier items. In a separate zip-sealable bag, add bag ingredient. Squeeze air out of bag, zip seal, and place bag in jar. Top jar with an oxygen packet for longer-term storage, cover with a new canning lid, and hand-tighten the metal ring.

Cooking directions: Remove oxygen packet and discard. Empty contents of jar into a 4-quart pot with 7 cups of water and simmer for 20–25 minutes. Add the bag ingredient and cook 10–12 minutes more until pasta is tender.

Estimated
Shelf Life
if stored in a cool, dry place

10–15
YEARS

Ode to D'Atri's
Minestrone

MEALS IN A JAR
FOR ONE

MEALS IN A JAR FOR ONE

I'm excited to share with you some of my favorite personal-sized meals I use to take with me for long work days, on-the-go lunches, and stays in hotel rooms. Oh yeah—the party travels with me! Truth be known, sometimes I just want something familiar when I travel, and I don't want it to be the familiar taste of fast food cheeseburgers. I started making personal-sized Meals in a Jar for me and the kids to have on the go. Initially it was for summer lunches for my boys with the bottomless-pit stomachs. Seriously, what is it with boys and constant eating?

TACO RICE FOR ONE

Use the instant rice in this recipe. It will cook in about five minutes and be a quick and savory meal on the run.

Estimated Shelf Life *if stored in a cool, dry place* 5–10 YEARS

Jar directions: Layer ingredients in a widemouthed pint-sized jar, shaking the dry powder ingredients into the bulkier items. Top with an oxygen packet for longer-term storage, cover with a new canning lid, and hand-tighten the metal ring.

Cooking directions: Remove oxygen packet and discard. Empty contents of the jar into a quart-sized pot with 2½ cups of boiling water. Turn off heat and cover pan. Let sit for 5–7 minutes until water is absorbed.

Jar ingredients:

¾ cup instant white rice

¼ cup Honeyville freeze-dried sausage or taco TVP

2 Tbsp. Honeyville freeze-dried bell peppers

2 tsp. onion powder

1 tsp. Chef Tess Southwest Fajita seasoning

2 tsp. dehydrated jalapeño (optional)

2 Tbsp. Honeyville tomato powder

¼ cup Honeyville freeze-dried cheddar cheese

Country Beef Stew for One

COUNTRY BEEF STEW FOR ONE

If you're ever camping up in the mountains and you want a taste of something right out of the Old West, sit on down to a warm bowl of this stew. It will fill you up and give you all the comfort of home.

Estimated
Shelf Life
if stored in a cool, dry place

10–15 YEARS

Jar directions: Layer ingredients in a widemouthed pint-sized jar, shaking the dry powder ingredients into the bulkier items. Top with an oxygen packet for longer-term storage, cover with a new canning lid, and hand-tighten the metal ring.

Cooking directions: Remove oxygen packet and discard. Combine contents of the jar in a quart-sized pot with 1½ cups water and bring to a boil. Reduce heat and simmer for 15–20 minutes until vegetables are tender.

Jar ingredients:

¼ cup Honeyville quick-cook red beans

¼ cup Honeyville freeze-dried mixed vegetables

¼ cup Honeyville freeze-dried diced beef

¼ cup Honeyville dehydrated diced potatoes

¼ cup Honeyville dehydrated onion

½ tsp. Chef Tess All-Purpose seasoning

1 Tbsp. all-purpose flour or cornstarch

FRENCH HAM AND ASPARAGUS SOUP FOR ONE

Estimated
Shelf Life
if stored in a cool, dry place

5–10 YEARS

Jar ingredients:

2 Tbsp. Honeyville
freeze-dried ham

2 Tbsp. Honeyville
freeze-dried corn

1 Tbsp. Honeyville
freeze-dried onion

1 Tbsp. Honeyville
freeze-dried celery

2 Tbsp. Honeyville
freeze-dried asparagus

¼ cup Honeyville instant
milk

1 Tbsp. Honeyville sour
cream powder

2 Tbsp. Honeyville
dehydrated diced
potatoes

2 Tbsp. Honeyville cheese
sauce powder

½ tsp. Chef Tess French
Provencal Essential
seasoning

I have a friend who took this meal with her in her luggage to Paris! She had rented an apartment there for her vacation and found this to be the perfect companion to a piece of Brie and some real French bread! I really wish she had taken me in her luggage instead of the soup. However, taking my soup with her was almost as good as having me there. . . . I'll keep telling myself that.

Jar directions: Layer ingredients in a widemouthed pint-sized jar, shaking the dry powder ingredients into the bulkier items. Top with an oxygen packet for longer-term storage, cover with a new canning lid, and hand-tighten the metal ring.

Cooking directions: Remove oxygen packet and discard. Bring 1½ cups of water to a boil in a 2-quart pot. Combine contents of the jar with boiling water. Reduce to low heat and simmer for 10–15 minutes until meat and vegetables are tender and soup is slightly thickened. Turn off heat and allow to sit an additional 5 minutes. Serve hot.

CHEF TESS'S TACO SOUP FOR ONE

This recipe includes chicken breast and has only 380 calories with 14 grams of fiber and only 8 grams of fat.

Estimated
Shelf Life
if stored in a cool, dry place

10–15 YEARS

Jar directions: Layer ingredients in a widemouthed pint-sized jar, shaking the dry powder ingredients into the bulkier items. Top with an oxygen packet for longer-term storage, cover with a new canning lid, and hand-tighten the metal ring.

Jar ingredients:

¼ cup Honeyville quick-cook red beans

¼ cup Honeyville taco TVP

¼ cup Honeyville freeze-dried chicken

1 Tbsp. Honeyville dehydrated onion

2 Tbsp. Honeyville freeze-dried bell peppers

¼ cup Honeyville freeze-dried corn

1 Tbsp. Honeyville tomato powder

¾ tsp. homemade taco seasoning

Cooking directions: Remove oxygen packet and discard. Combine contents of the jar in a quart-sized pot on the stove. Add 2½ cups of water and simmer for 10–15 minutes until veggies are tender. Serve with nacho chips, sour cream, and salsa if desired.

CHEF TESS'S AFRICAN SWEET POTATO CHICKEN STEW FOR ONE

Jar ingredients:

- 2 Tbsp. Honeyville dehydrated onion

- 1½ tsp. dehydrated minced garlic

- 1½ tsp. Chef Tess Gingham Masala*

- 2 Tbsp. Honeyville freeze-dried celery

- 2 Tbsp. Honeyville dehydrated carrots

- 1 Tbsp. Honeyville red bell pepper granules

- ¼ cup Honeyville freeze-dried sweet potatoes

- 1 tsp. MSG-free chicken bouillon

- ¼ cup Honeyville freeze-dried chicken (optional)

- 2 Tbsp. Honeyville powdered peanut butter

- 1½ tsp. dehydrated cilantro

- ⅓ cup Honeyville tomato powder

This is my go-to meal when I want a hot and savory soup with plenty of depth and character.

Jar directions: Layer ingredients in a pint-sized jar, shaking the dry powder ingredients into the bulkier items. Top with an oxygen packet for longer-term storage, cover with a new canning lid, and hand-tighten the metal ring.

Cooking directions: Remove oxygen packet and discard. In a pot with 2 cups of water, add contents of the jar. Simmer over low heat for 15–20 minutes.

*GINGHAM MASALA is a specialty blend of spices similar in flavor to tandoori masala. I made it to benefit impoverished HIV orphan children. We do this through education and providing healthy meals in India through the help of ginghamproject.org. This particular blend can be ordered online.

Estimated Shelf Life
if stored in a cool, dry place
5–10 YEARS

Chef Tess's African Sweet Potato Chicken Stew for One

HONEYVILLE CLASSIC CHILI FOR ONE

Estimated
Shelf Life
if stored in a cool, dry place

10–15 YEARS

Jar ingredients:

½ cup Honeyville quick-cook red beans

¼ cup tomato powder

¼ cup freeze-dried diced beef or chili-flavored TVP

1 Tbsp. dehydrated onion

2 Tbsp. freeze-dried bell peppers

1 Tbsp. Honeyville freeze-dried celery

¾ tsp. MSG-free beef bouillon

¾ tsp. chili powder (more or less depending on how you like your chili)

¾ tsp. Chef Tess All-Purpose seasoning

pinch of hot chili flakes (optional; if you like it hot)

I use a personal-sized lunch slow cooker when I travel to hotels. This chili always hits the spot and saves me money.

Jar directions: Layer ingredients in a widemouthed pint-sized jar, shaking the dry powder ingredients into the bulkier items. Top with an oxygen packet for longer-term storage, cover with a new canning lid, and hand-tighten the metal ring.

Cooking directions: Remove oxygen packet and discard. In a 1-quart pot, combine contents of the jar with 2 cups of hot water (more or less depending on how thick you like your chili). Simmer over medium-high heat for 10–15 minutes until it is rehydrated and ready to eat.

BREAKFAST

6-Grain Carrot Cake
Breakfast Pudding

6-GRAIN CARROT CAKE BREAKFAST PUDDING

My grandmother used to make an amazing old-fashioned carrot pudding for Thanksgiving. This breakfast cereal tastes like a cross between her pudding and a rich carrot cake. It's not as sweet as carrot cake or as dense as grandma's pudding, so add more sweetener if you prefer. I just drizzle this with some coconut milk and top it with toasted nuts. However you do it, I know this is going to be a family favorite!

Jar directions: Layer pineapple and carrots in a wide-mouthed quart-sized jar. Add powdered milk, butter, honey, flavorings, pudding mix, salt, and spice blend, and shake the dry ingredients into the bulkier items. Now add the 6-grain rolled cereal. The jar will be full. Top with an oxygen packet for longer-term storage, cover with a new canning lid, and hand-tighten the metal ring.

Cooking directions: Remove oxygen packet and discard. Bring 5 cups of water to a rolling boil. Add contents of the jar to the water and stir. Lower the heat to a simmer and cook for 10–12 minutes. Turn off the heat. Cover and let sit for 5 minutes (to be sure pineapple is hydrated). Serve warm. Drizzle with milk, honey, or syrup and top with any chopped nuts if desired.

Jar ingredients:

- ½ cup Honeyville freeze-dried pineapple or freeze-dried apples
- 1 cup Honeyville dehydrated carrot
- ½ cup Honeyville instant milk
- ¼ cup Honeyville powdered butter
- ½ cup Honeyville granulated honey or sugar
- 2 tsp. Mix-a-Meal coconut powder (optional)
- 1 Tbsp. Mix-a-Meal vanilla powder (optional)
- 2 Tbsp. Honeyville instant vanilla pudding mix
- ½ tsp. salt
- 1 tsp. Chef Tess Wise Woman of the East spice blend
- 2 cups Honeyville 6-grain rolled cereal

Estimated Shelf Life
if stored in a cool, dry place

5–10 YEARS

SAUSAGE GRAVY AND BISCUIT DUMPLINGS

Estimated Shelf Life
if stored in a cool, dry place
5–10 YEARS

Jar ingredients:

1 cup Honeyville freeze-dried sausage

½ cup Honeyville instant nonfat dry milk

½ cup Honeyville cream cheese powder

1 Tbsp. Honeyville dehydrated onion

1 tsp. Chef Tess All-Purpose seasoning

⅛ tsp. black pepper

¼ cup Honeyville all-purpose flour

Bag ingredients:

1 cup Honeyville all-purpose flour

1 tsp. baking soda

2 Tbsp. Honeyville buttermilk powder

¼ tsp. salt

Jar directions: Layer jar ingredients in a widemouthed quart-sized jar, shaking the dry powder ingredients into the bulkier items. In a zip-sealable bag, add all bag ingredients. Squeeze air out of bag, twist it sealed, and place on top of the jar ingredients. Top jar with an oxygen packet for longer-term storage, cover with a new canning lid, and hand-tighten the metal ring.

Cooking directions: Remove oxygen packet and discard. In a 12-inch deep skillet with a lid, combine the jar ingredients with 3 cups of hot water and bring to a simmer. Cook on medium heat for 10–12 minutes, stirring occasionally. In a medium bowl, combine the bag ingredients with ⅓ cup of cold water. Stir just until combined. Drop this biscuit batter into the gravy in the skillet in 5–6 equal mounds of dough. Cover skillet and reduce heat to a low simmer. Cook for 10–12 minutes until biscuits are cooked through.

PEANUT BUTTER CUP BREAKFAST CEREAL

I love the creamy peanut butter warm and gooey, dripping over the lightly sweet milk chocolate cereal with a hint of vanilla. It is a salty sweet taste of perfect peanut butter bliss.

Estimated Shelf Life
if stored in a cool, dry place
5–10 YEARS

Jar directions: Layer jar ingredients in a widemouthed quart-sized jar, shaking the dry powder ingredients into the bulkier items. In a zip-sealable bag, add bag ingredient. Squeeze air out of bag, twist it sealed, and place on top of the jar ingredients. Top jar with an oxygen packet for longer-term storage, cover with a new canning lid, and hand-tighten the metal ring

Cooking directions: Remove oxygen packet and discard. In a saucepan, combine jar ingredients with 1¼ cups of boiling water and cook for 3–4 minutes. (Or, microwave with 1¼ cups water for 2 minutes. Stir and cook 1 additional minute.) Mix peanut butter powder with 1 tablespoon of cool water and stir until smooth. Drizzle over hot cereal mixture. Serve hot.

Jar ingredients:

2 cups Honeyville 6-grain rolled cereal, pulsed in a food processor for 10–15 seconds

1 Tbsp. baker's cocoa

2 Tbsp. sugar or sugar alternative

½ tsp. vanilla powdered flavor

Bag ingredient:

1 cup Honeyville powdered peanut butter

SWEET POTATO AND CORN SKILLET FRITTATA

Jar ingredients:

½ cup Honeyville freeze-dried sausage

1 cup Honeyville freeze-dried sweet potato

½ cup Honeyville freeze-dried corn

½ cup Honeyville freeze-dried mushroom

½ cup Honeyville freeze-dried bell pepper

¼ cup Honeyville dehydrated onion

12 scoops (equal to 9 eggs) Honeyville Ova Easy egg crystals (1.3 oz.)

1 cup Honeyville freeze-dried Colby cheese

1 tsp. Chef Tess Southwest Fajita seasoning

½ tsp. dry oregano

½ tsp. fresh cracked pepper or ancho chili powder

2 Tbsp. Honeyville all-purpose flour

2 Tbsp. Honeyville instant milk

1 Tbsp. Honeyville powdered sour cream

Honeyville sweet potatoes are not yams. They are the traditional southern sweet white potatoes used in all the traditional dishes. Here in the southwest, we kick up our skillet frittatas with some heat!

Jar directions: Layer the sausage and veggies in a widemouthed quart-sized jar. Then add the eggs. Shake the dry ingredients into the bulkier items. Next add the cheese and remaining ingredients. Top with an oxygen packet for longer-term storage, cover with a new canning lid, and hand-tighten the metal ring.

Cooking directions: Remove oxygen packet and discard. In a 2-quart bowl, combine 3 cups of cool water and the contents of the jar and allow to hydrate for about 10 minutes. Whisk a couple of times after 5 minutes to be sure everything gets moist. Lightly oil a 10-inch skillet with a tightly fitting lid. Heat skillet on low for 2–3 minutes. Pour in hydrated mixture. Cover with tightly fitting lid and allow to cook for 15–17 minutes on very low. Turn off the heat, but do not uncover skillet. Allow to carry-over cook for 5–7 minutes. Remove lid and slice as you would a pizza. Serve warm with salsa of your choice.

Estimated Shelf Life
if stored in a cool, dry place
5–10 YEARS

Sweet Potato and Corn Skillet Frittata

SPICED MAPLE PEACHES AND CREAM RICE PUDDING

Estimated
Shelf Life
if stored in a cool, dry place

5 YEARS

Jar ingredients:

1 cup Honeyville long-grain rice

1 cup Honeyville instant milk

½ cup Honeyville peaches and cream smoothie mix

1 cup Honeyville freeze-dried peaches

2 tsp. maple powder

½ cup Honeyville instant vanilla pudding

Jar directions: Layer ingredients in a widemouthed, quart-sized jar, shaking the dry powder ingredients into the bulkier items. Top with an oxygen packet for longer-term storage, cover with a new canning lid, and hand-tighten the metal ring.

Cooking directions: Remove oxygen packet and discard. Empty jar contents into a saucepan with 5 cups of hot water. Bring to a boil. Reduce to a low simmer and cover with a tight lid. Simmer for 25–30 minutes, stirring every 5 minutes. Take off the heat and allow to sit for 5–10 minutes.

SPICED SAMOAN COCONUT CREAM FARINA WITH MANGO

This meal is made in a pint-sized jar. Farina is the same as Cream of Wheat but is less expensive.

Estimated Shelf Life
if stored in a cool, dry place

5 YEARS

Jar directions: Layer ingredients in a widemouthed pint-sized jar, shaking the dry powder ingredients into the bulkier items. Top with an oxygen packet for longer-term storage, cover with a new canning lid, and hand-tighten the metal ring.

Cooking directions: Remove oxygen packet and discard. Empty contents of jar into 4 cups of boiling water, whisking briskly until combined. Simmer for 3–4 minutes and serve hot, with toasted coconut if desired.

Jar ingredients:

(Use a pint-sized jar)

1 cup Honeyville farina

⅓ cup Honeyville Tropical Monsoon smoothie mix

⅓ cup Honeyville granulated honey

⅓ cup Honeyville freeze-dried mango

1 tsp. Mix-a-Meal pineapple powder

½ tsp. Chef Tess Wise Woman of the East spice blend

CARAMEL RASPBERRY CHOCOLATE TRUFFLE BREAKFAST PUDDING

Estimated
Shelf Life
if stored in a cool, dry place

5 YEARS

This meal is made in a pint-sized jar. Chocolate truffles for breakfast can only be a good idea, right? I might as well put "Just for Mom" in the title.

Jar ingredients:

(Use a pint-sized jar)

1 cup Honeyville farina

¼ cup Honeyville raspberry hot cocoa mix

¼ cup Honeyville Dutch baker's cocoa

⅓ cup Honeyville freeze-dried raspberries

1½ tsp. Mix-a-Meal butterscotch powder

⅓ cup Honeyville granulated honey or sugar

Jar directions: Layer ingredients in a pint-sized jar, shaking the dry powder ingredients into the bulkier items. Top with an oxygen packet for longer-term storage, cover with a new canning lid, and hand-tighten the metal ring.

Cooking directions: Remove oxygen packet and discard. Empty contents of jar into 4 cups of rapidly boiling water, whisking briskly until combined. Simmer for 3–4 minutes. Serve hot, with chocolate chips if desired.

GRANDMA'S BUTTERMILK CUSTARD BREAKFAST

One of the most delightful desserts I've ever enjoyed has come from the kitchen of my mother-in-law every Thanksgiving. It is a creamy and smooth buttermilk custard with a hint of spice. Hers is a pie, but the breakfast version makes me full of thanksgiving every single day!

Estimated Shelf Life
if stored in a cool, dry place
5–10 YEARS

Jar directions: Layer ingredients in a pint-sized jar, shaking the dry powder ingredients into the bulkier items. Top with an oxygen packet for longer-term storage, cover with a new canning lid, and hand-tighten the metal ring.

Cooking directions: Remove oxygen packet and discard. Combine dry ingredients with 2 cups of boiling water and cook for 3–4 minutes. (Or microwave with 1¼ cups of water for 2 minutes. Stir and cook 1 additional minute.) Serve hot.

Jar ingredients:

½ cup Honeyville buttermilk powder

½ cup sugar or Honeyville granulated honey

1 cup Honeyville farina

½ tsp. Chef Tess Wise Women of the East spice blend

2 tsp. lemon flavor powder

1 tsp. vanilla flavor powder

1 tsp. butterscotch flavor powder

Mom's Ham and Zucchini
Quiche Casserole

MOM'S HAM AND ZUCCHINI QUICHE CASSEROLE

Quiche casserole is basically a crustless breakfast casserole. This originated with my mother trying to use up a ton of zucchini from our garden. It has become one of our family favorites. With the technology now available to make crystallized eggs along with the freeze-dried meats and vegetables came the ability to turn a classic and adored family egg dish into a shelf-stable meal.

Jar directions: Layer ingredients in a widemouthed quart-sized jar, shaking the dry powder ingredients into the bulkier items. Add cheese last. Top with an oxygen packet for longer-term storage, cover with a new canning lid, and hand-tighten the metal ring.

Cooking directions: Remove oxygen packet and discard. Preheat the oven to 325°F. Pour the jar ingredients in a 2-quart bowl and add 2½ cups of cool water. Allow to hydrate for 10 minutes. Lightly grease a 9×9 casserole dish. Pour hydrated contents into dish and cover with foil. Bake until set, about 50 minutes. Do not overbake. May be stored in refrigerator after baking and heated for serving.

*NOTE: 2 tablespoons of regular cornstarch can be used in place of the ultra gel.

Estimated Shelf Life
if stored in a cool, dry place
5–10 YEARS

Jar ingredients:

- 2 Tbsp. Honeyville dehydrated green onion

- 1 cup Honeyville freeze-dried ham

- ½ cup Honeyville freeze-dried zucchini

- ½ cup Honeyville freeze-dried bell peppers

- 1 Tbsp. Honeyville powdered butter

- ¼ cup Honeyville Ova Easy egg crystals (no substitutions)

- ½ cup Honeyville powdered sour cream

- 2 Tbsp. ultra gel* (modified cornstarch)

- ½ tsp. Chef Tess Romantic Italian seasoning

- 1 cup Honeyville freeze-dried cheddar cheese

BLUEBERRY GINGERBREAD BREAKFAST BAKE

Estimated
Shelf Life
if stored in a cool, dry place

3–5 YEARS

Jar ingredients:

2 cups Honeyville freeze-dried blueberries

¼ cup Honeyville lemonade powder

2 Tbsp. cornstarch

Bag ingredients:

1 cup Honeyville all-purpose flour

1 tsp. baking soda

2 Tbsp. Honeyville buttermilk powder

½ cup Honeyville granulated honey

2 tsp. Chef Tess Wise Woman of the East spice blend

¼ tsp. salt

Jar directions: Layer jar ingredients in a widemouthed quart-sized jar, shaking the dry powder ingredients into the bulkier items. In a zip-sealable bag, add all bag ingredients. Squeeze air out of the bag, twist it sealed, and place on top of the jar ingredients. Top jar with an oxygen packet for longer-term storage, cover with a new canning lid, and hand-tighten the metal ring.

Cooking directions: Remove oxygen packet and discard. Preheat oven to 350°F. In a 10-inch oven-proof Dutch oven with a lid, combine the jar ingredients with 2 cups of warm water and stir well. Allow to hydrate for 10–15 minutes. Bring to a low simmer and cook until berries are completely tender and sauce begins to thicken. While berry mixture is cooking, combine the bag ingredients with ⅓ cup of cool water in a bowl, just until combined. Drop this batter in 6 equal mounds on top of berry mixture. Cover with a lid and bake for 12–15 minutes until gingerbread is cooked through (toothpick inserted into the cake comes out clean).

OVERLY EASY SAUSAGE VEGGIE OMELETS

Jar directions: Layer jar ingredients in a widemouthed quart-sized jar, shaking the dry powder ingredients into the bulkier items. In a zip-sealable bag, add bag ingredient. Squeeze air out of bag, twist it sealed, and place on top of the jar ingredients. Top jar with an oxygen packet for longer-term storage, cover with a new canning lid, and hand-tighten the metal ring.

Cooking directions: Remove oxygen packet and discard. In a medium bowl, combine jar ingredients with 4 cups of cool water. Allow to hydrate for 10 minutes. In a second bowl, lightly mist the cheese with a little cool water. In a medium nonstick skillet over medium heat, gently cook the omelets, 1 cup of mixture at a time. When cooked through, gently sprinkle each omelet with 2 tablespoons of the hydrated cheese. Yields 4 (8-inch) omelets.

Estimated Shelf Life
if stored in a cool, dry place
10–15 YEARS

Jar ingredients:

1 cup Honeyville freeze-dried sausage

1 cup Honeyville freeze-dried bell pepper

1 cup Honeyville Ova Easy egg crystals (no substitutions)

¼ cup Honeyville freeze-dried onions

½ cup Honeyville freeze-dried mushrooms

Bag ingredient:

½ cup Honeyville freeze-dried cheddar cheese

COUNTRY SAUSAGE, HASH BROWN, AND PEPPER-CHEESE SCRAMBLED EGG SKILLET

Estimated
Shelf Life
if stored in a cool, dry place

10 YEARS

Jar ingredients:

- 2 cups Honeyville dehydrated diced potatoes
- 1 cup Honeyville freeze-dried sausage (no substitutions)
- 1 tsp. Chef Tess All-Purpose seasoning

Bag ingredients:

- ⅓ cup Honeyville Ova Easy egg crystals (no substitutions)
- ⅓ cup Honeyville freeze-dried cheddar cheese
- ⅓ cup Honeyville freeze-dried bell peppers
- 2 Tbsp. Honeyville freeze-dried mushrooms
- ½ tsp. Chef Tess Romantic Italian seasoning

Have you ever been to a diner where they serve a generous portion of crispy potatoes and meat under a fluffy portion of scrambled cheesy eggs on a personal-sized skillet? This is the family-sized version! You won't need any extra oil because there is an ample amount in the freeze-dried sausage. Also, use egg crystals here—the texture is just like a regular scrambled egg!

Jar directions: Layer jar ingredients in a widemouthed quart-sized jar, shaking the dry powder ingredients into the bulkier items. In a zip-sealable bag, add all bag ingredients. Squeeze air out of bag, twist it sealed, and place on top of the jar ingredients. Top jar with an oxygen packet for longer-term storage, cover with a new canning lid, and hand-tighten the metal ring.

Cooking directions: Remove oxygen packet and discard.

POTATO DIRECTIONS: In a 12-inch nonstick skillet, combine the jar ingredients with 4 cups of boiling water. Cover and allow to hydrate for 10–15 minutes until potatoes are tender. Drain any extra water once the potatoes are tender. The fat from the sausage will keep the potatoes from sticking to the pan. Cook for 10–15 minutes over medium heat, stirring once or twice but allowing the potatoes to brown well.

EGG DIRECTIONS: In a quart-sized bowl, empty the contents of the bag into ⅔ cups of cool water, whisking well. Allow to hydrate for 5 minutes. In a small nonstick skillet on low heat, slowly cook the egg mixture for 3–5 minutes, stirring often. Serve eggs over the potato mixture.

Country Sausage, Hash Brown, and Pepper-Cheese Scrambled Egg Skillet

HAZELNUT DOUBLE CHOCOLATE TRUFFLE CUPS

Estimated
Shelf Life
if stored in a cool, dry place

5 YEARS

Jar ingredients:

1½ cups Honeyville 4-grain cereal or quick-cook oats

½ cup Honeyville hazelnut hot cocoa mix

2 Tbsp. Honeyville Dutch baker's cocoa

¼ tsp. salt

2 tsp. butterscotch flavor powder

Jar directions: Layer ingredients in a pint-sized jar. Top with an oxygen packet for longer-term storage, cover with a new canning lid, and hand-tighten the metal ring.

Cooking directions: Remove oxygen packet and discard. Combine jar ingredients with 4 cups of boiling water and cook for 3–4 minutes. Serve hot. You may top with chopped chocolate if desired.

VANILLA AND ORANGE ROLL CEREAL CUPS

In one of the church congregations I attended, there was a gorgeous gal named Yvonne who made some killer-amazing orange rolls. She'd use them warm from the oven as bribery to get people to come out to choir practice—and it worked like a charm. Everyone asked for the recipe, yet she never shared it. I love her dearly for still sharing the rolls. Here's a variation on that amazing flavor . . . for your breakfast cereal!

Estimated Shelf Life *if stored in a cool, dry place* — **5–10 YEARS**

Jar ingredients:

1¼ cups Honeyville 4-grain cereal mix

½ cup Honeyville vanilla pudding powder

¼ cup Honeyville granulated honey

2 tsp. dehydrated granulated orange zest*

Jar directions: Layer ingredients in a widemouthed pint-sized jar. Top with an oxygen packet for longer-term storage, cover with a new canning lid, and hand-tighten the metal ring.

Cooking directions: Remove oxygen packet and discard. Combine contents of the jar with 2½ cups of boiling water in a saucepan. Simmer for 3–4 minutes. Use more or less water depending on how thick or thin you like your cereal.

*GRANULATED ORANGE ZEST is available in most grocery stores in the baking aisle. To make your own, zest an orange. Place zest in a food dehydrator on a fine mesh screen and allow to dry for 4–5 hours on low. Grind to a fine powder in a spice mill.

4-GRAIN BUTTERSCOTCH BANANA MUFFIN CUPS

Estimated
Shelf Life
if stored in a cool, dry place

10–15 YEARS

This hot cereal tastes like a fresh-from-the-oven banana muffin! I'm fond of drizzling my muffins in honey or butterscotch sauce. This is as close as you can get to these muffins without getting your fingers sticky!

Jar ingredients:

- 1⅓ cup Honeyville 4-grain cereal or quick oats

- ½ cup Honeyville granulated honey

- 2 tsp. butterscotch flavor powder

- ¾ cup Honeyville freeze-dried bananas

Jar directions: Layer ingredients in a widemouthed quart-sized jar, shaking the dry powder ingredients into the bulkier items. Top with an oxygen packet for longer-term storage, cover with a new canning lid, and hand-tighten the metal ring.

Cooking directions: Remove oxygen packet and discard. Combine contents of the jar with 2⅔ cups of boiling water. Simmer for 3–4 minutes. Use more or less water depending on how thick or thin you like you cereal.

9-GRAIN PEACHES AND CREAM COBBLER CEREAL

Warm chunks of peach enshrouded in a creamy smooth cereal that tastes like a fresh-baked cobbler is sure to please on any cold morning! Try it with a hot cup of Honeyville hazelnut hot cocoa. It is bliss.

Estimated Shelf Life
if stored in a cool, dry place
5–10 YEARS

Jar directions: Layer ingredients in a widemouthed pint-sized jar, shaking the dry powder ingredients into the bulkier items. Top with an oxygen packet for longer-term storage, cover with a new canning lid, and hand-tighten the metal ring.

Cooking directions: Remove oxygen packet and discard. In a saucepan, bring 4 cups of water to a boil. Add in contents of the jar. Simmer over low heat for 10–12 minutes.

Jar ingredients:

1 cup Honeyville 9-grain cereal

¾ cup Honeyville freeze-dried peaches

½ cup Honeyville peaches and cream smoothie mix

1 tsp. Chef Tess Wise Woman of the East spice blend

Savory Onion and Herb
Potato Cakes with Sausage

SAVORY ONION AND HERB
POTATO CAKES WITH SAUSAGE

When I was a kid, my sweet dad would use leftover mashed potatoes as the base for delicious skillet potato cakes. I'd always look forward to that meal! In this recipe, the addition of sausage and buttermilk makes it a classic.

Estimated Shelf Life
if stored in a cool, dry place

5–10 YEARS

Jar directions: Layer ingredients in a widemouthed, quart-sized jar, shaking the dry powder ingredients into the bulkier items. Top with an oxygen packet for longer-term storage, cover with a new canning lid, and hand-tighten the metal ring.

Cooking directions: Remove oxygen packet and discard. In a bowl, add the jar ingredients and then 5 cups of hot water. Stir well and cool for 10 minutes. Oil a medium skillet and spoon the potato mixture onto the skillet in 8 patties. Flatten and cook over medium heat for 5 minutes. Lightly turn the potato cakes and cook for an additional 3–5 minutes. Serve warm.

Jar ingredients:

2 cups Honeyville potato flakes

1 cup Honeyville freeze-dried sausage

¾ cup Honeyville Ova Easy egg crystals

1 Tbsp. Honeyville freeze-dried onions

2 Tbsp. Honeyville buttermilk powder

1 tsp. baking soda

1 tsp. Chef Tess All-Purpose seasoning

BERRIES AND BAVARIAN LEMON CREAM CEREAL

Estimated Shelf Life
if stored in a cool, dry place

5–10 YEARS

There's something so right when we can have a decadent dessert for breakfast. Here's a flavor combination that will satisfy your sweet tooth without compromising you waistline.

Jar ingredients:

- 1 cup Honeyville 4-grain cereal mix or quick-cook oats
- ¼ cup flax seeds
- ¾ cup Honeyville freeze-dried berries of your choice (I crush them up a bit before I measure them)
- ¼ cup Honeyville wild berry smoothie mix
- 2 Tbsp. Honeyville lemonade powder

Jar directions: Layer ingredients in a widemouthed pint-sized jar, shaking the dry powder ingredients into the bulkier items. Top with an oxygen packet for longer-term storage, cover with a new canning lid, and hand-tighten the metal ring.

Cooking directions: Remove oxygen packet and discard. In a saucepan, boil 2⅔ cups of water and add contents of the jar. Simmer for 3–4 minutes. Use more or less water depending on how thick or thin you like you cereal.

BREAKFAST
FOR ONE

CHEESY SCRAMBLED EGGS
WITH SAUSAGE FOR ONE

Estimated
Shelf Life
if stored in a cool, dry place

**10–15
YEARS**

It is sometimes hard to find a higher protein punch for the morning, but this personal-sized scrambled egg combination is one that works! It is also great for those who are diabetic and need higher protein options in their food storage. Use a half-pint jar for a personal serving.

Jar ingredients:

- ¼ cup Honeyville Ova Easy egg crystals (no substitution)

- 1 Tbsp. Honeyville cheese sauce powder

- ¼ cup Honeyville freeze-dried sausage

- ¼ tsp. Chef Tess All-Purpose seasoning

Jar directions: Layer ingredients in a half-pint-sized jar, shaking the dry powder ingredients into the bulkier items. Top with an oxygen packet for longer-term storage, cover with a new canning lid, and hand-tighten the metal ring.

Cooking directions: Remove oxygen packet and discard. Combine contents of the jar with 1 cup of water. Simmer for 3–4 minutes. Cook on a hot skillet for 3–4 minutes.

**Cheesy Scrambled Eggs
with Sausage for One**

4-Grain Cereal for One

4-GRAIN CEREAL FOR ONE

Use this 4-grain cereal recipe base and then choose one of the flavor variation recipes from the next few pages. It will be just what you need to get going in the morning. One serving stored in a half-pint jar is perfect for when I want to have breakfast in a convenient container ready to add boiling water and enjoy! Cost effective, nutritious, and outstandingly tasty!

Jar directions: Layer ingredients in a half-pint-sized jar, shaking the dry powder ingredients into the bulkier items. Top with an oxygen packet for longer-term storage, cover with a new canning lid, and hand-tighten the metal ring.

Cooking directions: Remove oxygen packet and discard. Combine contents of the jar with ½ cup of boiling water. Simmer for 3–4 minutes. Use more or less water depending on how thick or thin you like your cereal.

Estimated Shelf Life
if stored in a cool, dry place
5–10 YEARS

Jar ingredients:

- ⅓ cup Honeyville 4-grain cereal mix
- 1 Tbsp. Honeyville oat bran or ground flax seed

BERRIES AND BAVARIAN LEMON CREAM CEREAL FOR ONE

Jar directions: Layer ingredients in a half-pint-sized jar, shaking the dry powder ingredients into the bulkier items. Top with an oxygen packet for longer-term storage, cover with a new canning lid, and hand-tighten the metal ring.

Cooking directions: Remove oxygen packet and discard. Combine contents of the jar with ½ cup of boiling water. Simmer for 3–4 minutes. Use more or less water depending on how thick or thin you like your cereal.

Estimated shelf life: 5–10 years.

Jar ingredients:

- 4-grain cereal base (see above)
- 3 Tbsp. freeze-dried berries of your choice (I crush them up a bit before I measure them)
- 2 Tbsp. Honeyville wild berry smoothie mix
- 1 tsp. Honeyville lemonade powder

SPICED PEACHES AND CREAM
COBBLER CEREAL FOR ONE

Jar ingredients:

4-grain cereal base (p. 131)

3 Tbsp. Honeyville
freeze-dried peaches

2 Tbsp. Honeyville peaches
and cream smoothie mix

¼ tsp. Chef Tess Wise
Woman of the East
spice blend

Jar directions: Layer ingredients in a half-pint-sized jar, shaking the dry powder ingredients into the bulkier items. Top with an oxygen packet for longer-term storage, cover with a new canning lid, and hand-tighten the metal ring.

Cooking directions: Remove oxygen packet and discard. Combine contents of the jar with ½ cup of boiling water. Simmer for 3–4 minutes. Use more or less water depending on how thick or thin you like your cereal.

Estimated shelf life: 5–10 years.

MAPLE-CRANBERRY PECAN
CEREAL FOR ONE

Jar ingredients:

4-grain cereal base (p. 131)

2 Tbsp. Honeyville
dehydrated honey

¼ tsp. Mix-a-Meal maple
powder

3 Tbsp. chopped toasted
pecans

2 Tbsp. Honeyville dried
cranberries

Jar directions: Layer ingredients in a half-pint-sized jar, shaking the dry powder ingredients into the bulkier items. Top with an oxygen packet for longer-term storage, cover with a new canning lid, and hand-tighten the metal ring.

Cooking directions: Remove oxygen packet and discard. Combine contents of the jar with ½ cup of boiling water. Simmer for 3–4 minutes. Use more or less water depending on how thick or thin you like your cereal.

Estimated shelf life: 2–3 years.

SPICED VANILLA-ORANGE CEREAL FOR ONE

Jar directions: Layer ingredients in a half-pint-sized jar, shaking the dry powder ingredients into the bulkier items. Top with an oxygen packet for longer-term storage, cover with a new canning lid, and hand-tighten the metal ring.

Cooking directions: Remove oxygen packet and discard. Combine contents of the jar with ½ cup of boiling water. Simmer for 3–4 minutes. Use more or less water depending on how thick or thin you like your cereal.

Estimated shelf life: 10–15 years.

Jar ingredients:

4-grain cereal base (p. 131)

¼ tsp. Chef Tess Wise Woman of the East spice blend

2 Tbsp. Honeyville vanilla pudding powder

1 Tbsp. Honeyville dehydrated honey

½ tsp. dry orange zest (or ¼ tsp. Mix-a-Meal orange powder)

....

BANANA BREAD CEREAL FOR ONE

Jar directions: Layer ingredients in a half-pint-sized jar, shaking the dry powder ingredients into the bulkier items. Top with an oxygen packet for longer-term storage, cover with a new canning lid, and hand-tighten the metal ring.

Cooking directions: Remove oxygen packet and discard. Combine contents of the jar with ½ cup of boiling water. Simmer for 3–4 minutes. Use more or less water depending on how thick or thin you like your cereal.

Estimated shelf life: 10–15 years.

Jar ingredients:

4-grain cereal base (p. 131)

3 Tbsp. Honeyville dehydrated honey

1 tsp. Mix-a-Meal butterscotch powder

3 Tbsp. Honeyville freeze-dried banana

½ tsp. almond flavor powder

TROPICAL WHITE CHOCOLATE
MACADAMIA NUT CEREAL FOR ONE

Jar ingredients:

4-grain cereal base (p. 131)

2 Tbsp. Honeyville Tropical
Monsoon smoothie mix

1 Tbsp. white chocolate
chips

1 Tbsp. chopped macadamia
nuts

Jar directions: Layer ingredients in a half-pint-sized jar, shaking the dry powder ingredients into the bulkier items. Top with an oxygen packet for longer-term storage, cover with a new canning lid, and hand-tighten the metal ring.

Cooking directions: Remove oxygen packet and discard. Combine contents of the jar with ½ cup of boiling water. Simmer for 3–4 minutes. Use more or less water depending on how thick or thin you like your cereal.

Estimated Shelf Life: Up to 2 years with macadamia nuts.

ORANGE-GLAZED CRANBERRY CARROT PUDDING FOR ONE

If we can have chocolate truffles for breakfast (p. 112), then certainly there is room for carrot cake, especially if it is packed with shredded carrots and nine grains!

Estimated Shelf Life
if stored in a cool, dry place
3 YEARS

Jar directions: To keep glaze separate for a topper, place ingredients in a snack-size zip bag. In a second zip-seal bag, place the cranberries. Layer remaining ingredients in a pint-sized jar, shaking the dry powder ingredients into the bulkier items. Add the two zip-sealed baggies. Top with an oxygen packet for longer-term storage, cover with a new canning lid, and hand-tighten the metal ring.

Cooking directions: Remove oxygen packet and discard. In a saucepan, bring 3 cups of water to a boil. Empty contents of jar into water and cook on high for 10–15 minutes. Mix orange glaze ingredients with 1 tablespoon of cool water and stir until smooth. Sprinkle dried cranberries over hot cereal mixture and drizzle with glaze.

Jar ingredients:

¼ cup Honeyville dehydrated shredded or diced carrots

¾ cup Honeyville 9-grain cereal mix

¼ cup Honeyville granulated honey

½ tsp. Chef Tess Wise Women of the East spice blend

¼ tsp. almond flavor powder

¼ tsp. salt

Bag ingredients for glaze:

½ cup powdered sugar

¼ tsp. orange powder

Second bag ingredients:

½ cup dehydrated orange-infused cranberries

STRAWBERRIES AND CREAM FARINA FOR ONE

Estimated
Shelf Life
if stored in a cool, dry place

5–10
YEARS

Jar ingredients:

¼ cup Honeyville farina

2 Tbsp. Honeyville
strawberry milk alternative

2 Tbsp. Honeyville
freeze-dried strawberries

1 tsp. Honeyville powdered
butter

½ tsp. vanilla flavor powder

2 Tbsp. sugar

Jar directions: Layer ingredients in a pint-sized jar, shaking the dry powder ingredients into the bulkier items. Top with an oxygen packet for longer-term storage, cover with a new canning lid, and hand-tighten the metal ring.

Cooking directions: Remove oxygen packet and discard. In a saucepan, combine contents of the jar with 1 cup of boiling water. Stirring constantly, cook for 3–4 minutes. Simmer for 2–3 minutes until thickened.

Strawberries and Cream
Farina for One

6-GRAIN DOUBLE CHOCOLATE HAZELNUT TRUFFLE CEREAL FOR ONE

Estimated
Shelf Life
if stored in a cool, dry place

5 YEARS

Jar ingredients:

½ cup 6-grain cereal

2 Tbsp. Honeyville hazelnut
hot cocoa mix

1 tsp. baker's cocoa powder

pinch of salt

½ tsp. Mix-a-Meal
butterscotch powder

Jar directions: Layer ingredients in a pint-sized jar, shaking the dry powder ingredients into the bulkier items. Top with an oxygen packet for longer-term storage, cover with a new canning lid, and hand-tighten the metal ring.

Cooking directions: Remove oxygen packet and discard. Combine contents of the jar with 1¼ cups boiling water. Simmer for 3–4 minutes. Use more or less water depending on how thick or thin you like your cereal. Try topping it with chopped chocolate.

GRANDMA'S BUTTERMILK BREAKFAST CUSTARD FOR ONE

This single-serving meal is enough for a teenage boy (or 2 adults).

Estimated Shelf Life
if stored in a cool, dry place

5 YEARS

Jar directions: Layer ingredients in a pint-sized jar, shaking the dry powder ingredients into the bulkier items. Top with an oxygen packet for longer-term storage, cover with a new canning lid, and hand-tighten the metal ring.

Cooking directions: Remove oxygen packet and discard. Combine contents of the jar with 2 cups of boiling water in a saucepan. Simmer for 3–4 minutes. Use more or less water depending on how thick or thin you like it.

Jar ingredients:

⅓ cup Honeyville powdered buttermilk

¼ cup sugar

½ cup Honeyville farina

¼ tsp. Chef Tess Wise Woman of the East spice blend

¼ tsp. Mix-a-Meal lemon powder

½ tsp. Mix-a-Meal vanilla powder

½ tsp. Mix-a-Meal butterscotch powder

6-GRAIN PEANUT BUTTER CUP BREAKFAST FOR ONE

Estimated Shelf Life

if stored in a cool, dry place

5 YEARS

Jar ingredients:

- ½ cup Honeyville 6-grain rolled cereal, pulsed in a food processor for 10–15 seconds

- 1 Tbsp. baker's cocoa

- 2 Tbsp. sugar or sugar alternative

- ½ tsp. Mix-a-Meal vanilla powder

Bag ingredient:

- ¼ cup Honeyville peanut butter powder

Jar directions: Layer ingredients in a pint-sized jar, shaking the dry powder ingredients into the bulkier items. Put bag ingredient in a snack baggie and twist closed. Top with an oxygen packet for longer-term storage, cover with a new canning lid, and hand-tighten the metal ring.

Cooking directions: Remove oxygen packet and discard. Combine contents of the jar with 1¼ cups of boiling water. Simmer for 3–4 minutes. Use more or less water depending on how thick or thin you like your cereal. Mix peanut butter powder with 1 tablespoon of cool water and stir until smooth. Drizzle over hot cereal, with chopped chocolate if desired.

9-GRAIN SPICED APPLE PIE CEREAL FOR ONE

Jar directions: Layer jar ingredients in a pint-sized jar, shaking the dry powder ingredients into the bulkier items. Top with an oxygen packet for longer-term storage, cover with a new canning lid, and hand-tighten the metal ring.

Cooking directions: Remove oxygen packet and discard. Combine contents of the jar with 1 cup of boiling water in a saucepan. Simmer for 10–15 minutes until tender, stirring occasionally. Cover pot and allow fruit to rehydrate for about 2 minutes.

Estimated Shelf Life
if stored in a cool, dry place

5–10 YEARS

Jar ingredients:

¼ cup Honeyville 9-grain cereal

1 Tbsp. Honeyville powdered butter

2 Tbsp. Honeyville nonfat powdered milk

2 Tbsp. sugar

¼ tsp. Chef Tess Wise Woman of the East spice blend

¼ cup Honeyville freeze-dried apples

BREADS

BREAD IN A JAR

I n planning my Meals in a Jar menu, I usually plan on two or more loaves of bread a day for my family. I've found my favorite way to pack the ingredients is in a premeasured recipe in a jar. If you bake often, this is a great method for keeping everything in one location. For these jars, where I'm packing the yeast in the jar, I use the commercially made yeast packets for ease. If you want to make your own, use a snack bag with 2 teaspoons of instant yeast. I've included some of my favorite breads and rolls in this section. Enjoy.

6-GRAIN BREAD

Jar directions: Layer ingredients in a quart-sized jar. Top with an oxygen packet for longer-term storage, cover with a new canning lid, and hand-tighten the metal ring.

Estimated Shelf Life
if stored in a cool, dry place
3–5 YEARS

Cooking directions: Remove oxygen absorber and discard. Combine the jar ingredients with the contents of the yeast packet and 1⅓ cups of cool water. (If you use whole wheat flour, you will need 2 cups of water depending on how dry the flour is). Knead for 3–5 minutes by hand. Put dough in an ungreased gallon-sized bowl and allow it to rise, covered, for 1½–2 hours. Form into a loaf and place in a greased 8-inch loaf pan. Allow to rise 1 hour or until doubled in size. Preheat oven to 425°F. Bake for 15 minutes. Reduce heat to 350°F and bake for 20 minutes.

Jar ingredients:

2 Tbsp. Honeyville instant potato flakes

2 Tbsp. Honeyville granulated honey or sugar

¼ cup Honeyville instant nonfat dry milk

½ tsp. salt

½ cup Honeyville 6-grain flour

2½ cups Honeyville California Best bread flour or Honeyville Alta artisan bread flour

1 packet instant yeast

Onion Dill Rolls

ONION DILL ROLLS

Jar directions: Layer ingredients in a quart-sized jar. Top with an oxygen packet for longer-term storage, cover with a new canning lid, and hand-tighten the metal ring.

Estimated Shelf Life
if stored in a cool, dry place

3–5 YEARS

Cooking directions: Remove oxygen absorber and discard. Combine jar ingredients with yeast packet and 1⅓ cups of cool water. Knead for 3–5 minutes by hand. Put dough in an ungreased gallon-sized bowl and allow to rise, covered, for 1½–2 hours. Form into 8–10 large rolls of equal size and place in a greased 9×13 baking pan. Allow to rise for 1 hour or until doubled in size. Preheat oven to 425°F. Bake for 20–25 minutes.

Jar ingredients:

2 Tbsp. Honeyville instant potato flakes

2 Tbsp. Honeyville granulated honey or sugar

2 Tbsp. Honeyville instant dry milk or soy milk

1 Tbsp. Honeyville freeze-dried onions

2 tsp. Chef Tess The Big Dill seasoning

½ tsp. salt

3½ cups Honeyville baker's high-gluten bread flour

1 packet instant yeast

CLASSIC HONEY WHEAT BREAD

Estimated
Shelf Life
if stored in a cool, dry place

3–5 YEARS

Jar ingredients:

2 Tbsp. Honeyville vital wheat gluten

½ cup Honeyville granulated honey

½ tsp. salt

3¼ cups Honeyville Ultra Grain or Mountain Mills whole wheat flour

1 packet instant yeast

Jar directions: Layer ingredients in a quart-sized jar. Top with an oxygen packet for longer-term storage, cover with a new canning lid, and hand-tighten the metal ring.

Cooking directions: Remove oxygen absorber and discard. Combine jar ingredients with yeast packet and 2⅓ cups of cool water. Knead for 3–5 minutes by hand. Put dough in an ungreased gallon-sized bowl and allow to rise, covered, for 1½–2 hours. Form into a loaf and place in a greased 8-inch loaf pan. Allow to rise for 1 hour or until doubled in size. Preheat oven to 425°F. Bake for 15 minutes. Reduce heat to 350°F and bake for 20 minutes.

CLASSIC WHITE BREAD

Jar directions: Layer ingredients in a quart-sized jar. Top with an oxygen packet for longer-term storage, cover with a new canning lid, and hand-tighten the metal ring.

Estimated Shelf Life
if stored in a cool, dry place

3–5 YEARS

Cooking directions: Remove oxygen absorber and discard. Combine jar mix with instant yeast and 1⅓ cups of cool water. Knead for 3–5 minutes by hand. Put dough in an ungreased gallon-sized bowl and allow to rise, covered, for 1½–2 hours. Form into a loaf and place in a greased 8-inch loaf pan. Allow to rise for 1 hour or until doubled in size. Preheat oven to 425°F. Bake for 15 minutes. Reduce heat to 350°F and bake for 20 minutes.

Jar ingredients:

- 2 Tbsp. Honeyville instant potato flakes
- 2 Tbsp. Honeyville granulated honey or sugar
- ¼ cup Honeyville instant dry milk or soy milk powder
- ½ tsp. salt
- 3½ cups Honeyville California Best bread flour or Honeyville Alta artisan bread flour
- 1 packet instant yeast

ROASTED RED PEPPER GARLIC ROLLS

Estimated
Shelf Life
if stored in a cool, dry place

3–5 YEARS

Jar ingredients:

2 Tbsp. Honeyville instant potato flakes

2 Tbsp. Honeyville granulated honey or sugar

3 Tbsp. dehydrated granulated red bell pepper flakes*

2 tsp. Chef Tess Romantic Italian seasoning

½ tsp. salt

1 tsp. granulated garlic

3½ cups Honeyville baker's high-gluten bread flour

1 packet instant yeast

Jar directions: Layer ingredients in a quart-sized jar. Top with an oxygen packet for longer-term storage, cover with a new canning lid, and hand-tighten the metal ring.

Cooking directions: Remove oxygen absorber and discard. Combine jar ingredients with yeast packet and 1⅓ cups of cool water. Knead for 3–5 minutes by hand. Put dough in an ungreased gallon-sized bowl and allow to rise, covered, for 1½–2 hours. Form into 8–10 large rolls of equal size and place in a greased 9×13 baking pan. Allow to rise for 1 hour or until doubled in size. Preheat oven to 425°F. Bake for 20–25 minutes.

*DEHYDRATED GRANULATED BELL PEPPER FLAKES
are available online at firehousepantrystore.com.

Roasted Red Pepper
Garlic Rolls

Honeyville Scones

HONEYVILLE SCONES

I grew up in the state of Utah, where scones are a chewy yeast-raised flat-bread that is deep-fried and drizzled with butter and honey. I know. It is heaven on earth. I don't deep-fry often any more—it is a special occasion when I do! For that reason, this is the only recipe in this book that will require the use of additional oil for the preparation of the finished product. I couldn't figure how to fit half gallon of oil in a quart jar. If you decide you don't want to deep-fry the scones, this mix makes excellent Greek-style pita bread as well!

Estimated
Shelf Life
if stored in a cool, dry place   2–3
YEARS

Jar ingredients:

3 cups Honeyville premium
    gourmet scone mix

¼ oz. packet of dry active
    yeast

Jar directions: Layer ingredients in a quart-sized jar. Top with an oxygen packet for longer-term storage, cover with a new canning lid, and hand-tighten the metal ring.

Cooking directions: Remove oxygen absorber and discard. Dissolve yeast packet into 1 cup of lukewarm water. Add scone mix and knead until a smooth dough is formed, about 3 minutes. Place dough in a bowl and allow to rise for 20 minutes. Roll dough to ¼ inch thick. Cut scones to desired shapes. Fry in 375-degree vegetable oil in a heavy Dutch oven until light golden-brown on each side. Serve warm with honey or topping of your choice.

Greek-style pita bread: Divide dough into 6 circles and roll ¼ inch thick on a lightly floured surface. In a thick-bottomed 12-inch skillet, cook the pita bread over medium-low heat, 3–4 minutes on each side.

TORTILLAS

Estimated
Shelf Life
if stored in a cool, dry place

3–5 YEARS

Jar ingredients:

2½ cups flour

1½ tsp. salt

1 tsp. baking soda

1 tsp. vinegar powder

½ tsp. garlic powder
(optional)

½ tsp. ground cumin
(optional)

½ tsp. ground oregano
(optional)

1 cup Honeyville
shortening powder

Jar directions: Layer ingredients in a quart-sized jar. Top with an oxygen packet for longer-term storage, cover with a new canning lid, and hand-tighten the metal ring.

Cooking directions: Remove oxygen absorber and discard. Empty jar ingredients into a bowl. Bring 1 cup of water to a boil. Dump boiling water into the flour mixture and combine using a heavy wooden spoon. Remove dough from the bowl and form into 6 balls, depending on the size of the tortillas you want. Roll into flat, round circles on a lightly floured counter until very thin. Cook tortillas on a hot 12-inch skillet, 2–3 minutes on each side.

DESSERTS

MIXED BERRY COBBLER

Estimated
Shelf Life
if stored in a cool, dry place

3—5
YEARS

Jar ingredients:

1 cup Honeyville
   freeze-dried blueberries

½ cup Honeyville
   freeze-dried strawberries

½ cup Honeyville
   freeze-dried blackberries

2 Tbsp. Honeyville lemonade
   mix

¼ cup ultra gel

1 tsp. almond powder flavor

Bag ingredients:

1 cup Honeyville buttermilk
   pancake mix

2 Tbsp. Honeyville
   strawberry milk alternative

2 Tbsp. Honeyville
   powdered butter

½ tsp. dehydrated lime zest

Jar directions: Layer jar ingredients in a widemouthed quart-sized jar, shaking the dry powder ingredients into the bulkier items. In a zip-sealable bag, add bag ingredients. Squeeze air out of bag, twist it sealed, and place on top of the jar ingredients. Top jar with an oxygen packet for longer-term storage, cover with a new canning lid, and hand-tighten the metal ring.

Filling directions: Combine the jar ingredients with 2 cups of water in a saucepan. Mix well. Simmer over low heat for 10 minutes until fruit is tender and mixture is thick. Allow to cool for about 10 minutes.

Topping directions: In a medium bowl, mix the bag ingredients with ⅓ cup of water just until combined. Do not overmix.

Cooking directions: Preheat oven to 350°F. Put the thickened filling mixture in a 1-quart casserole dish. Drop the cobbler topping mixture on the fruit mixture. Bake for 30–35 minutes until golden.

Mixed Berry Cobbler

GINGERED MANGO PEACH CRISP

Estimated
Shelf Life
if stored in a cool, dry place

5–10 YEARS

Jar ingredients:

- 1 cup Honeyville freeze-dried peaches
- 1 cup Honeyville freeze-dried mango
- 2 Tbsp. Honeyville lemonade mix
- ¼ cup ultra gel
- 1 tsp. Chef Tess Wise Woman of the East spice blend
- 1 tsp. finely minced candied ginger

Bag ingredients:

- 1 cup Honeyville quick-cook oats
- ⅓ cup sugar or sugar alternative
- ½ cup Honeyville powdered butter

Jar directions: Layer jar ingredients in a widemouthed quart-sized jar, shaking the dry powder ingredients into the bulkier items. In a zip-sealable bag, add bag ingredients. Squeeze air out of the bag, twist it sealed, and place on top of the jar ingredients. Top jar with an oxygen packet for longer-term storage, cover with a new canning lid, and hand-tighten the metal ring.

Filling directions: Combine jar ingredients with 2 cups of water in a saucepan. Mix well. Simmer over low heat for 10 minutes until fruit is tender and mixture is thick. Allow to cool for about 10 minutes.

Topping directions: In a medium bowl, combine bag ingredients with ¼ cup of water until a crumbly mixture is made.

Cooking directions: Preheat oven to 350°F. Put the thickened filling mixture in a 1-quart casserole dish. Drop the topping mixture on the fruit mixture. Bake for 30–35 minutes until golden.

CLASSIC CINNAMON COFFEE CAKE

Jar directions: Layer jar ingredients in a widemouthed quart-sized jar, shaking the dry powder ingredients into the bulkier items. In a zip-sealable bag, add bag ingredients. Squeeze air out of bag, twist it sealed, and place on top of the jar ingredients. Top with an oxygen packet for longer-term storage, cover with a new canning lid, and hand-tighten the metal ring.

Estimated Shelf Life
if stored in a cool, dry place
5 YEARS

Baking directions: Remove oxygen absorber and discard. Preheat oven to 325°F. Combine jar ingredients with 1½ cups of water and stir just until combined. Pour batter into a lightly greased 9-inch cake pan. Sprinkle bag ingredients over the batter. Bake for 30–35 minutes until golden brown and a toothpick inserted into the cake comes out clean. Serve warm.

Jar ingredients:

- 2¼ cups Honeyville Sno-King cake flour
- ½ cup sugar
- ½ cup Honeyville powdered buttermilk
- 1 tsp. baking soda
- 1 tsp. almond flavor powder
- ¼ cup Honeyville powdered whole eggs

Bag ingredients:

- ¼ cup Honeyville powdered butter
- ¼ cup sugar
- 1 Tbsp. Chef Tess Wise Woman of the East spice blend

Apple Pie Bake

APPLE PIE BAKE

Apple pie is the ultimate comforting dessert. I like this recipe because it has one top crust and is baked much like a cobbler. The lemonade powder in the filling gives it a kiss of tartness.

Estimated Shelf Life
if stored in a cool, dry place
3–5 YEARS

Jar directions: Layer jar ingredients in a widemouthed quart-sized jar, shaking the dry powder ingredients into the bulkier items. In a zip-sealable bag, add bag ingredients. Squeeze air out of bag, twist it sealed, and place on top of the jar ingredients. Top jar with an oxygen packet for longer-term storage, cover with a new canning lid, and hand-tighten the metal ring.

Crust directions: Combine bag ingredients with ¼ cup of cold water and mix, just until combined. Allow to sit for 5 minutes. Roll the dough between two pieces of parchment paper into a 9-inch circle. Set aside.

Filling directions: Preheat oven to 425°F. Combine the jar ingredients with 2 cups of cool water. Allow to hydrate for 10 minutes. Pour into a 9-inch pie plate or 8-inch cake pan. Top with crust. Flute the edges if desired. Poke a few slits into the crust and bake for 25–30 minutes until golden brown.

Jar ingredients:

2½ cups Honeyville freeze-dried apples

¼ cup Honeyville lemonade powder

1 tsp. Chef Tess Wise Woman of the East spice blend

¼ cup ultra gel (no substitutions)

Bag ingredients:

¾ cup Honeyville all-purpose flour

½ cup Honeyville shortening powder

¼ tsp. salt

MOM'S EMERGENCY
CHOCOLATE MELTDOWN CAKE

Estimated
Shelf Life
if stored in a cool, dry place

2–3 YEARS

Jar ingredients:

1 cup Honeyville all-purpose flour

½ cup sugar

¼ cup Honeyville hazelnut hot cocoa mix

¼ tsp. salt

1½ tsp. baking soda

¼ cup Honeyville powdered butter

Bag ingredients:

¾ cup sugar

¼ cup Honeyville baker's cocoa

If Mom doesn't have something in the food storage for her chocolate addiction, then there is sure to be some terror on the home front . . . and it won't be an atom bomb. It will be Mom. Okay, it might not be that bad, but every single mom on earth who loves chocolate should make sure there's a supply of chocolate pudding cake mixes on hand for the times when nothing but chocolate will do to satisfy your craving.

Jar directions: Layer jar ingredients in a widemouthed quart-sized jar, shaking the dry powder ingredients into the bulkier items. In a zip-sealable bag, add bag ingredients. Squeeze air out of bag, twist it sealed, and place on top of the jar ingredients. Top jar with an oxygen packet for longer-term storage, cover with a new canning lid, and hand-tighten the metal ring.

Cooking directions: Remove oxygen absorber and discard. Preheat oven to 350°F. Combine jar ingredients with ½ cup of water and stir until just combined. Grease an 8-inch cake pan and pour cake batter into the pan. In a bowl, combine the bag ingredients with ⅓ cup of boiling water to make the glaze. Stir until smooth. Pour the pudding glaze over the cake batter in the pan. Bake in center of the oven for 35–40 minutes. If topping with ice cream, invert cake onto a 10-inch plate while cake is still warm . Or scoop cake from the pan like a cobbler.

Mom's Emergency
Chocolate Meltdown Cake

BUTTERMILK APRICOT CUSTARD BAKE

Estimated
Shelf Life
if stored in a cool, dry place

5–10 YEARS

Jar ingredients:

1 cup Honeyville
freeze-dried apricots

1 cup sugar

3 Tbsp. cornstarch

½ cup Honeyville powdered
buttermilk

½ cup Honeyville Ova Easy
egg crystals

½ cup Honeyville powdered
butter

1 tsp. vanilla flavor powder

dash of nutmeg

Buttermilk custard pie is a tradition at our house that was started by my mother-in-law. This is a crustless version that also includes the addition of apricot.

Jar directions: Layer jar ingredients in a widemouthed quart-sized jar, shaking the dry powder ingredients into the bulkier items. Top with an oxygen packet for longer-term storage, cover with a new canning lid, and hand-tighten the metal ring.

Cooking directions: Remove oxygen absorber and discard. Preheat oven to 325°F. In a medium bowl, combine jar ingredients with 2½ cups of cool water. Whisk well. Pour into a lightly oiled 8-inch cake pan. Bake for about 35 minutes, until a knife inserted into the custard comes out clean.

OLD-FASHIONED STRAWBERRY SHORTCAKE

Jar directions: Layer jar ingredients in a widemouthed quart-sized jar, shaking the dry powder ingredients into the bulkier items. In a zip-sealable bag, add bag ingredients. Squeeze air out of bag, twist it sealed, and place on top of the jar ingredients. Top jar with an oxygen packet for longer-term storage, cover with a new canning lid, and hand-tighten the metal ring.

Cooking directions: Remove oxygen absorber and discard. Preheat oven to 425°F. Combine bag ingredients with ⅓ cup of cold water and mix just until combined. Roll out into an 8-inch square and cut into 6 squares of equal size. Place on a lightly greased sheet pan and bake 12–15 minutes. Combine the jar ingredients with 2 cups of cool water and mix well. Allow to thicken while shortcakes bake. Serve strawberry mixture over shortcake.

Estimated Shelf Life *if stored in a cool, dry place* **3–5 YEARS**

Jar ingredients:

- 2½ cups Honeyville freeze-dried strawberries
- ¼ cup sugar
- 1 tsp. strawberry Kool-Aid powder (optional)
- ¼ cup ultra gel (no substitutions)

Bag ingredients:

- 1 cup Honeyville all-purpose flour
- ⅓ cup sugar
- 3 Tbsp. Honeyville buttermilk powder
- ¼ tsp. salt
- 1 tsp. baking soda
- 1 tsp. vanilla powder flavoring

Lemon Cream Custard
with Gingerbread Bites

LEMON CREAM CUSTARD WITH GINGERBREAD BITES

Jar directions: Layer jar ingredients in a widemouthed quart-sized jar, shaking the dry powder ingredients into the bulkier items. In a zip-sealable bag, add bag ingredients. Squeeze air out of bag, twist it sealed, and place on top of the jar ingredients. Top with an oxygen packet for longer-term storage, cover with a new canning lid, and hand-tighten the metal ring.

Gingerbread directions: Remove oxygen packet and discard. Preheat oven to 350°F. Combine bag ingredients with ½ cup of cold water and mix well. Drop dough by 12 rounded tablespoons onto an ungreased cookie sheet, about 1 inch apart. Bake for 10–12 minutes until golden brown.

Custard directions: In a large bowl, combine jar ingredients with 1½ cups of ice water and whisk until fluffy, about 3 minutes.

*For a no-sugar-added version, substitute ½ cup of Honeyville granular erythritol plus 2 tsp True Lemon crystallized lemon for the lemonade powder.

Estimated Shelf Life
if stored in a cool, dry place
2–3 YEARS

Jar ingredients:

- ½ cup Honeyville lemonade powder*
- ¼ cup ultra gel (no substitutions)
- 1½ cup Honeyville cream cheese powder

Bag ingredients:

- ¾ cup 6-grain or whole wheat pastry flour
- ¼ cup Honeyville granulated honey or coconut sugar
- ½ cup Honeyville powdered butter
- ½ tsp. baking soda
- ¼ tsp. salt
- 1 tsp. Chef Tess Wise Woman of the East spice blend

LEMON POPPY SEED CAKE
WITH BLUEBERRY COMPOTE

Estimated
Shelf Life
if stored in a cool, dry place

5 YEARS

Jar ingredients:

2¼ cups Honeyville Sno-King cake flour

½ cup sugar

1 tsp. baking soda

2 Tbsp. Honeyville lemonade powder

1 Tbsp. poppy seeds

1 tsp. almond flavor powder

¼ cup Honeyville powdered whole eggs

Bag ingredients:

1 cup Honeyville freeze-dried blueberries

¼ cup Honeyville lemonade powder

¼ cup ultra gel (no substitutions)

Jar directions: Layer jar ingredients in a widemouthed quart-sized jar, shaking the dry powder ingredients into the bulkier items. In a zip-sealable bag, add bag ingredients. Squeeze air out of bag, twist it sealed, and place on top of the jar ingredients. Top jar with an oxygen packet for longer-term storage, cover with a new canning lid, and hand-tighten the metal ring.

Cooking directions: Remove oxygen absorber and discard. Preheat oven to 325°F. Combine jar ingredients with 1½ cups of water. Mix until just combined. Pour into a lightly oiled 8-inch cake pan and bake at 30–35 minutes. Place bag ingredients in a medium bowl. Add 1½ cups of boiling water and allow it to sit for 15–20 minutes until berries are hydrated. Serve over the cake.

PINEAPPLE UPSIDE-DOWN CAKE WITH CARAMEL SAUCE

Jar directions: Layer jar ingredients in a widemouthed quart-sized jar, shaking the dry powder ingredients into the bulkier items. In a zip-sealable bag, add bag ingredients. Squeeze air out of bag, twist it sealed, and place on top of the jar ingredients. Top with an oxygen packet for longer-term storage, cover with a new canning lid, and hand-tighten the metal ring.

Cooking directions: Remove oxygen absorber and discard. Preheat oven to 325°F. Combine bag ingredients with 1 cup boiling water and stir well. Allow to hydrate 15 minutes until pineapple is tender. In a large bowl, combine jar ingredients with 1½ cups of cool water. Mix just until combined. Pour the pineapple mixture into the bottom of a 9-inch by 3-inch-deep round cake pan. Top with batter and spread out to the edge of the pan. Bake for 30–35 minutes until toothpick inserted into the cake comes out clean. Remove from the oven and immediately invert the cake onto a serving dish. Serve warm.

Estimated Shelf Life *if stored in a cool, dry place* — **3–5 YEARS**

Jar ingredients:

- 2¼ cups Honeyville cake flour
- ½ cup sugar
- 1 tsp. baking soda
- 2 Tbsp. Honeyville powdered buttermilk
- 1 tsp. almond flavor powder
- ¼ cup Honeyville powdered whole eggs

Bag ingredients:

- 1 cup Honeyville freeze-dried pineapple
- ¼ Honeyville granulated honey or coconut sugar
- ¼ cup Honeyville powdered butter
- 2 tsp. butterscotch flavor powder

LEMON-LIME CHEESECAKE PIE

Estimated
Shelf Life
if stored in a cool, dry place

5 YEARS

Jar ingredients:

⅓ cup lime gelatin powder

1½ cups Honeyville cream cheese powder

¾ cup Honeyville Insta-Whip topping mix

Bag ingredients:

¾ cup Honeyville 6-grain flour

½ cup Honeyville shortening powder

¼ tsp. salt

Jar directions: Layer jar ingredients in a widemouthed quart-sized jar, shaking the dry powder ingredients into the bulkier items. In a zip-sealable bag, add bag ingredients. Squeeze air out of bag, twist it sealed, and place on top of the jar ingredients. Top with an oxygen packet for longer-term storage, cover with a new canning lid, and hand-tighten the metal ring.

Cooking directions: Remove oxygen absorber and discard. Preheat oven to 425°F. Combine bag ingredients with ¼ cup of cold water. Mix just until combined and allow to sit for 5 minutes. Bring 2½ cups of water to a boil. In a large metal bowl, combine the jar ingredients with the boiling water and stir for 3–5 minutes until gelatin crystals are dissolved. Set aside. Roll pie crust between two sheets of parchment paper into a 10-inch circle. Line a 9-inch pie pan with the crust and bake for 15–20 minutes until golden brown. While crust bakes, chill filling in the fridge for 20 minutes. Remove crust from the oven and allow to cool on a wire rack. Remove filling from fridge. Whip with an electric mixer for 5 minutes on medium-high until fluffy. Pour into cooled crust. Chill for 2 hours until set.

Lemon-Lime
Cheesecake Pie

MISSISSIPPI MUD FUDGE BROWNIES

Estimated Shelf Life
if stored in a cool, dry place

2–3 YEARS

Jar ingredients:

- 2 cups Honeyville fudge brownie mix

- 2 Tbsp. Honeyville powdered whole eggs

- ½ cup Honeyville powdered butter

- 1 cup dark chocolate chips

Jar directions: Layer jar ingredients in a widemouthed quart-sized jar. Top with an oxygen packet for longer-term storage, cover with a new canning lid, and hand-tighten the metal ring.

Baking directions: Remove oxygen absorber and discard. Preheat oven to 350°F. Combine jar ingredients with ½ cup of water and stir just until combined. Pour batter into an 8×8 pan and bake for 20–25 minutes.

HOLIDAY
COOKIE MIXES

HOLIDAY COOKIE MIXES IN A JAR

Is it just me, or does the holiday season come too quickly? It seems like there's always one thing or another that needs to be done or baked or delivered. The joy of giving can easily be lost in the hustle. But it doesn't need to be that way. I get a jump start on all the gifts by making a few of these handy cookie mixes ahead of time. That way, I don't ever feel too stressed. These are fabulous in pint- or quart-sized jars (depending on the size of the recipe) and will be shelf stable for two to three years with an oxygen absorber. Wow! Right?

CHEF TESS'S EXTRA-MOIST BUTTERMILK COOKIES

This moist and chewy cookie mix can save you a ton of money on holiday neighbor gifts and can be made into multiple cookie mixes simply by adding a few different ingredients! See the next few pages for variations.

Estimated Shelf Life
if stored in a cool, dry place
2–3 YEARS

To make cookie mix: Combine all ingredients well. This mix will make approximately 20 cups of cookie mix. Use 2 cups of mix per jar or bag (or the amount specified for the flavor variations). This recipe will fill 10 bags or 10 quart-sized jars (when using add-in recipes).

Jar directions: Place 2 cups of the cookie mix in a widemouthed quart-sized jar. Top with an oxygen packet for longer-term storage, cover with a new canning lid, and hand-tighten the metal ring.

To bake as buttermilk sugar cookies: Remove oxygen absorber and discard. Combine cookie mix with ⅓ cup of water and stir well. Place 1-inch balls on a cookie sheet and bake at 350°F for 10–12 minutes. Yields 1 dozen cookies.

Jar ingredients:

9 cups Honeyville all-purpose flour

1¼ cup Honeyville powdered whole eggs

1 cup Honeyville powdered buttermilk

1½ cup Honeyville vanilla pudding mix

2 Tbsp. baking soda

1 Tbsp. salt

4 cups Honeyville powdered butter

3½ cups sugar or Honeyville granulated honey

Raspberry
Cocoa-Coated Crinkles

RASPBERRY COCOA–COATED CRINKLES

Jar directions: Place 2 cups of the cookie mix in a widemouthed quart-sized jar. In a zip-sealable bag, add bag ingredient. Squeeze air out of the bag, twist it sealed, and place on top of the jar ingredients. Top jar with an oxygen packet for longer-term storage, cover with a new canning lid, and hand-tighten the metal ring.

Estimated Shelf Life
if stored in a cool, dry place
2–3 YEARS

Jar ingredients:

2 cups buttermilk cookie mix (p. 175)

1 tsp. LorAnn raspberry-flavored oil, combined well with the cookie mix

Bag ingredient:

½ cup Honeyville raspberry hot cocoa mix

Baking directions: Remove oxygen absorber and discard. Combine jar ingredients with ⅓ cup water and stir well. Form dough into 12 (1-inch) balls and roll each cookie in the raspberry cocoa mix. Place balls on a cookie sheet and bake at 350°F for 8–10 minutes.

MINT COCOA BROWNIE BITES

Estimated
Shelf Life
if stored in a cool, dry place

2–3 YEARS

Jar directions: Layer jar ingredients in a widemouthed quart-sized jar. Top with an oxygen packet for longer-term storage, cover with a new canning lid, and hand-tighten the metal ring.

Jar ingredients:

2 cups buttermilk cookie mix (p. 175)

¼ cup Honeyville Dutch baker's cocoa

3 level scoops Honeyville mint hot cocoa mix

½ cup sugar

1 cup chocolate chips

Baking directions: Remove oxygen absorber and discard. Combine jar ingredients with ⅓ cup of water and stir well. Form dough into 12 (1-inch) balls. Flatten lightly. Place balls on a cookie sheet and bake at 350°F for 8–10 minutes.

4-GRAIN CARAMEL APPLE WALNUT COOKIES

Jar directions: Layer jar ingredients in a widemouthed quart-sized jar, shaking the dry powder ingredients into the bulkier items. Top with an oxygen packet for longer-term storage, cover with a new canning lid, and hand-tighten the metal ring.

Baking directions: Remove oxygen absorber and discard. Combine jar ingredients with ⅓ cup of water and stir well. Form dough into 12 (1-inch) balls. Flatten lightly. Place balls on a cookie sheet and bake at 350°F for 8–10 minutes.

Estimated Shelf Life
if stored in a cool, dry place

2–3 YEARS

Jar ingredients:

1 cup Honeyville 4-grain cereal or quick rolled oats

1 cup buttermilk cookie mix (p. 175)

½ cup sugar

½ cup Honeyville freeze-dried apples

½ cup chopped walnuts

2 tsp. butterscotch flavor powder

ELVIS'S BLUE CHRISTMAS PEANUT BUTTER AND BANANA WHOOPIE PIES

Estimated Shelf Life
if stored in a cool, dry place
2–3 YEARS

Jar ingredients:

2 cups buttermilk cookie mix (p. 175)

1 cup Honeyville powdered peanut butter

½ cup sugar

2 tsp. Mix-a-Meal banana powder

Bag ingredients:

1 cup powdered sugar

¼ cup cocoa

½ tsp. vanilla flavor powder

Jar directions: Place jar ingredients in a widemouthed quart-sized jar. In a zip-sealable bag, add bag ingredients. Squeeze air out of the bag, twist it sealed, and place on top of the jar ingredients. Top jar with an oxygen packet for longer-term storage, cover with a new canning lid, and hand-tighten the metal ring.

Baking directions: Remove oxygen absorber and discard. Combine cookie mix with ⅓ cup of water and stir well. Form dough into 12 (1-inch) balls. Flatten lightly. Place balls on a cookie sheet and bake at 350°F for 8–10 minutes. For frosting, combine bag ingredients with 1½ tablespoons of very hot water. (Use more or less water depending on how thick you want the frosting.) Spread the frosting on one peanut butter cookie and top with another cookie.

Elvis's Blue Christmas Peanut
Butter and Banana Whoopie Pies

CREAMY WHITE CHOCOLATE EGGNOG COOKIES

Estimated
Shelf Life
if stored in a cool, dry place

2–3 YEARS

Jar ingredients:

2 cups buttermilk cookie mix (p. 175)

½ cup sugar

¼ cup Honeyville cream cheese powder

½ tsp. Wise Woman of the East spice blend

1 cup white chocolate chips

Jar directions: Layer jar ingredients in a widemouthed quart-sized jar, shaking the dry powder ingredients into the bulkier items. Top with an oxygen packet for longer-term storage, cover with a new canning lid, and hand-tighten the metal ring.

Baking directions: Remove oxygen absorber and discard. Preheat oven to 350°F. Combine jar ingredients with ⅓ cup of water and stir well. Scoop dough by rounded tablespoons onto a lightly greased baking sheet. Bake at 350°F for 8–10 minutes. Allow cookies to cool for 5 minutes before removing from baking pan.

HAWAIIAN CHRISTMAS COOKIES

Jar directions: Layer jar ingredients in a widemouthed quart-sized jar, shaking the dry powder ingredients into the bulkier items. Top with an oxygen packet for longer-term storage, cover with a new canning lid, and hand-tighten the metal ring.

Baking directions: Remove oxygen absorber and discard. Preheat oven to 350°F. Combine jar ingredients with ¼ cup of water and stir well. Scoop dough by the rounded tablespoons onto a lightly greased baking sheet. Bake at 350°F for 8–10 minutes. Allow cookies to cool for 5 minutes before removing from baking pan.

*You can substitute with coconut flakes, but best if lightly pulsed 1 cup at a time in a dry blender until fine.

Estimated Shelf Life
if stored in a cool, dry place
2–3 YEARS

Jar ingredients:

1 cup buttermilk cookie mix (p. 175)

1 cup Honeyville macaroon coconut*

¼ cup sugar

1 tsp. coconut flavor powder

1 tsp. pineapple flavor powder

DARK CHOCOLATE CHIP
ORANGE-BRANDY COOKIES

**Estimated
Shelf Life**
if stored in a cool, dry place

**2–3
YEARS**

Jar ingredients:

2 cups buttermilk cookie mix
(p. 175)

½ cup sugar

1 tsp. LorAnn orange
brandy–flavored oil

2 tsp. butterscotch flavor
powder

1 cup dark chocolate chips,
72 percent cocoa

Jar directions: Layer jar ingredients in a widemouthed quart-sized jar. Top with an oxygen packet for longer-term storage, cover with a new canning lid, and hand-tighten the metal ring.

Baking directions: Remove oxygen absorber and discard. Preheat oven to 350°F. Combine cookie mix with ⅓ cup of water and stir well. Scoop by rounded tablespoons onto a lightly greased baking sheet. Bake at 350°F for 8–10 minutes. Allow cookies to cool for 5 minutes before removing from baking pan.

INDEX

ABOUT THE AUTHOR

Stephanie Petersen (a.k.a. Chef Tess Bakeresse) is a classically trained chef. She lives in Phoenix, Arizona, with her husband and two children. She has worked in bakeshops, restaurants, and banquets. When she became a mother in 1999, she set aside her work in the restaurant and focused full-time on her children. At the time, it seemed like such a sacrifice. Ironically, it became preparation for a much higher work. This time away from her career gave her real-world experience not only in cooking on a tight budget but also learning nutrition and gardening skills. When her church leader asked her to teach some of the gals some basic cooking skills, she soon found that she adored helping others grasp the basics that would help them save money and eat nutritional meals. She started milling her own spice blends late at night to earn extra money so she could be home with her babies.

When her youngest son started school in the fall of 2008, she started cheftessbakeresse.com—her food blog—with a borrowed cheap camera and no idea what she was getting into. It only took a few months before her unique talents with decorative bread and bread-painting techniques were noticed and published in *Australian Baking Business* magazine. Just a few months later, she was asked by the Fox 10 Arizona Morning Show if she would be a guest on the show. Thinking it would be a one-time visit, Stephanie went to the TV station. To her astonishment and joy, she has been a regularly featured chef since then and loves getting in front of the camera! It wasn't long after that first Fox 10 visit that she was also asked to be a regular guest chef and "Idea Extraordinaire" on NBC 12's Phoenix "Valley Dish," with ratings that beat Oprah when she was featured.

Stephanie has been a large group and personal cooking instructor since 2004 and continues to be heavily involved with culinary education around the country. One of her favorite places to teach is, of course, the Honeyville Farms retail stores. Stephanie's spices have been bottled by Honeyville Farms, and she feels deeply honored to write this Honeyville cookbook. She can often be found repeating her favorite words to her students, "Onward and upward, my friends!"